Appraising teachers in schools

The Editor

Les Bell is Senior Lecturer in Education at the University of Warwick. He has taught in primary and secondary schools, and at Coventry College of Education (now part of the University of Warwick). He regularly works in schools as a consultant and teaches on in-service management courses for teachers. He is co-author (with Peter Maher) of *Leading a Pastoral Team* (Blackwell, 1986).

Contributors

Francis Arnold, Les Bell, Kingsley Bungard, Clive Carthew, Harry Moore, Jenny Morris, A.J. Richardson, C.D.M. Rhodes, S.M. Slater, Norman Thomas

Routledge Education Books

Advisory editor: John Eggleston
Professor of Education
University of Warwick

Appraising teachers in schools

A practical guide

Edited by

Les Bell

Routledge
London

First published in 1988 by
Routledge
a division of Routledge, Chapman and Hall
11 New Fetter Lane, London EC4P 4EE

© Les Bell 1988

Set in 10/11 pt Times by
Columns of Reading
and printed in Great Britain by
Richard Clay Ltd., Bungay, Suffolk.

British Library Cataloguing in Publication Data
Appraising teachers in schools: a practical
  guide. – (Routledge education books).
  1. Great Britain. Schools. Teachers.
  Performance. Assessment
  I. Bell, Les
  371.1'44'0941

ISBN: 0–415–01301–1

Contents

v

Contents

Figures

List of Figures

Chapter 1

Appraisal and the Search for Accountability

Les Bell

This book is written for teachers. It is written for those teachers who are responsible for planning and implementing formal staff appraisal procedures and for those who may, in the future, share such a responsibility. It is also written for teachers who will experience staff appraisal in one or more of its many forms. In one sense, therefore, it is for all teachers since the new *Pay and Conditions of Employment* (DES, 1987) indicate that all teachers may be required to take part in some form of staff appraisal. Not only is this book for teachers but it is also based on the practical experience of teachers. All the chapters, with the exception of the first two and the last one, are written either by teachers who have experience in appraisal or about the experiences of such teachers. All the contributors have practical experience in evaluation and appraisal and, in particular, in the application of appraisal processes to schools. The book is a way of sharing those practical experiences in the hope that colleagues might benefit from them.

The work described was carried out by a range of people in a variety of institutions. Not only were the institutions different but the relationship of the writers to their institutions varied. Some are the headteachers or deputy headteachers, while others are external consultants invited to work with the teachers in the schools. This range of activities reflects the rich variety of approaches to staff appraisal which can be found in schools. It also reflects the extent to which the most appropriate and effective form of staff appraisal is that which is derived from, and rooted in, the particular circumstances of each school. Staff appraisal processes must take into account the uniqueness of each school and the individuality of teachers within that school. No attempt has been made, therefore, to suggest that there is only one workable model of staff appraisal. Indeed the various experiences described here exhibit significant differences, although they also have key features in common. The differences, the common features, and a series of general principles, which might be deduced from the practical approaches to staff appraisal on which this book is based, will all be discussed in the final chapter. Chapter one sets the scene for the practical examples of the introduction of staff appraisal into schools which follow. It seeks to examine those factors which have produced this interest in the appraisal of teachers. It explores a range of different meanings which can be attached to staff appraisal, some of which are more helpful than others. It seeks to place in context those processes which are discussed in subsequent chapters.

In search of accountability

The appraisal of teachers in schools is a process which is as old as the education service itself, although the nature of the process and the criteria used have changed over time. Grace (1985) has argued that 'gentleness and piety' were preferred to 'cleverness' by the early inspectors of schools. Such ideological reliability, which was embodied in religious and moral expressions of respectability, was soon linked to performance indicators. The first question asked by those responsible for managing schools or appointing teachers was: 'What percentage did you pass last year? Upon what is the salary and the reputation of a teacher to depend? Upon his ability to turn out so many yards of reading, writing and arithmetic from his human machines . . . ' (Gautney, 1937, p.119 quoted in Grace, 1985, p.8.)

Thus the ethics of industry, expressed in terms of measured production and close managerial control, were applied to schools more than a century ago. As a response to this teachers developed their own association to struggle for professional autonomy. By 1926, the claim of teachers to be professional and for schools to be relatively autonomous institutions was being taken seriously, if only to create a buffer against socialist ideas. As White has argued, ' . . . it was no longer in the interests of anti-Socialists, including Conservatives, to keep curriculum policy in the hands of the state . . . the Conservatives had everything to gain and nothing to lose from taking curricula out of the politicians' hands.' (White, 1975, p.28 quoted in Grace, 1985, p.11.)

What was intended here was that a system of controls over education would be created which was mediated through the professionalism of teachers. One of the effects of this process was to devolve evaluation and appraisal of teachers to headteachers while, at the same time, creating a climate which made open, formal performance assessment extremely difficult since the ethic of legitimated professionalism was based on teacher autonomy. This, in turn, presupposed individual self-evaluation and self-regulation by teachers themselves. Perhaps understandably, therefore, being a 'good professional', having an acceptable personality and establishing good social relations were esteemed qualities and the procedures used to assess these qualities were general, diffuse and less than systematic (Grace, 1978). Thus teachers applying for posts and asking for references were often unclear about the criteria upon which they would be judged and unsure about how the information would be collected. This situation still pertains in many schools.

In 1976, James Callaghan made his Ruskin College speech. The argument he put forward was partly a response to the then current criticism of education, and partly a means of raising a series of concerns about the extent to which the school curriculum was appropriate for the last quarter of the twentieth century. In particular, it raised the issues of the need for a core curriculum for all pupils; the need to pay more attention to the requirements of industry and to develop more positive attitudes towards industry on the part of young people; and the need to develop stronger links between schools and the wider society in order that the great secret garden, the curriculum, could come under public scrutiny. In order for this to happen teachers had to become more accountable to interest groups outside the school, including parents and industrialists. Thus, as Nisbet (1986) has argued, the accountability movement and the pressure for formal teacher appraisal is a challenge to the claim for autonomy by the teaching profession. This challenge is specific to education in the sense that it is an attempt to assert the right of non-professionals to have their views about education taken into account. It is also part of a more general challenge to professional autonomy for, as Leigh (1979) has argued, professions are suspected of a conspiracy against the laity.

Teachers who shelter behind 'the protective barrier of professionalism' (Nisbet, 1980, p.12) are also more difficult to manage and this at a time when the need to manage the teaching force more effectively was being identified by successive Secretaries of State for Education and Science. In 1977 Shirley Williams argued in her Green Paper, quoted in *The Times Educational Supplement*, that if the education service was to give value for money, then, a high priority had to be given to, 'The establishment of standard procedures for advice and, where necessary, warning to teachers whose performance is considered unsatisfactory' (*TES*, 9.11.84, p.7).

By 1983, Sir Keith Joseph was arguing that those managing schools had a clear responsibility to establish a policy for staff development based on the assessment of every teacher's performance (DES, 1983). This heralded what has been called, 'the Government's managerialist strategy for developing the statutory phase of schooling' (Wilcox, 1986, p.1). This was followed, early in 1984, with the statement that every LEA should have accurate information about each of its teachers and that such information should be based on, among other things, an assessment of the teacher's classroom performance (Joseph, 1984). This point was reaffirmed a year later when the Secretary of State asserted that the LEA can only be satisfied that each school is properly staffed if it knows enough about the competences of the individual teachers. Such knowledge could only come from some form of appraisal (Joseph, 1985). The White Paper *Better Schools* (DES, 1985a) gave notice that the Secretary of State would seek new powers to ensure that such appraisal schemes could be imposed on teachers if this became necessary. In 1986, Kenneth Baker, successor to Keith Joseph as Secretary of State for Education, piloted his new Education Act through Parliament. Contained within its strange miscellany of provision was the enabling legislation to which his predecessor had referred. This legislation is now embodied in *The Education (School Teachers' Pay and Conditions of Employment) Order 1987*, which imposed, for the first time, detailed conditions of service on teachers. These include, for headteachers:

(8a)   Supervising and participating in any arrangements within an agreed national framework, for the appraisal of the performance of teachers who teach in the School (Schedule 1, DES, 1987).

and for all other teachers:

(4)   Participating in any arrangements within an agreed

4

national framework for the appraisal of his performance and
that of other teachers (Schedule 3, DES 1987).

Thus it appears that the appraisal of teachers' performance is
with us in spirit, if not in action. Teachers are, in ways as yet
unclear, to be held accountable for their professional practices.

Responses to the search for accountability

The movement towards the appraisal of teacher performance is
only one part of what seems to be a set of strategies for changing
the nature of education provided in our schools. These strategies
include an attempt to restructure and revise the curriculum. This
can be traced through publications such as *A Framework for the
School Curriculum* (DES, 1979b), *The School Curriculum* (DES,
1981a) and *Circular 6/81*. In this each LEA was instructed to:

(a) review its policy for the school curriculum in its areas, and
    its arrangements for making that policy known to all
    concerned;
(b) review the extent to which current provision in the schools
    is consistent with that policy; and
(c) plan future developments accordingly, within the resources
    available.
    (DES, 181b, Circular 6/81, Section 5.)

. The *Curriculum from 5 to 16* series followed, number 2 of
which sought to promote professional discussion about the whole
curriculum in terms of breadth, balance, relevance and differentiation (DES, 1985c). At the same time, a number of initiatives
were taken that were intended to influence both curriculum
content and pedagogy. These included the introduction of new
technology to all sectors of education, and the development of the
Technical and Vocational Education Initiatives (TVEI) which
were funded by the MSC. The school curriculum now seems to
be about to experience an even more significant shift with the
proposed introduction of a national curriculum. The implications
of this for staff appraisal will be explored in chapter two.

Implicit in this re-analysis of the curriculum has been a re-
examination of forms of assessment and a debate about processes
of assessment. For example Bates (1984) has argued that
formative, criterion-referenced, diagnostic and teacher-made
forms of assessment may well serve 'educational' purposes more

5

faithfully than summative, norm-referenced, performance-based and standardized tests. These, he argues, are more closely related to 'managerial' purposes of sorting, classifying, allocating and controlling pupils. The Assessment of Performance Unit has been active in trying to identify criterion-referenced assessment processes across the curriculum while the pupil-profiling and the GCSE have added impetus to such developments. The proposed introduction of 'bench-mark' testing for all children at 7, 11 and 14 years of age will bring this aspect of education into the limelight yet again, although it remains to be seen how far the worst fears of the teaching profession about the stultifying and regimenting effects of these tests are realized.

The trend towards the appraisal of teachers, therefore, needs to be seen in the context of a series of other, perhaps related, changes in education. These changes may not all be taking us in the same direction. For example, there seems to be some significant contradictions in the emphasis on cross-curriculum, integrated approaches to teaching contained in, say, TVEI and CPVE (Certificate of Pre-Vocational Education), and the strong subject emphasis which, it appears, will pervade the national curriculum. As will be argued below, similar contradictions can be identified in the various sets of meanings which can be and have been attached to staff appraisal during the debate about its appropriateness for use in schools.

This debate is part of a broader reconsideration of the management of the teaching force. The extent to which teachers should be accountable and the identification of 'for what' and 'to whom' they should be accountable have been crucial aspects of this debate. These issues have not been settled but the role of the school governors in the accountability process has been considerably enhanced by the *1986 Education Act* while LEAs have had thrust upon them a more active role in managing the curriculum. This may soon change yet again if schools are given the opportunity to become financially autonomous or even to opt out of the LEA framework entirely. For the present there has been a significant devolution of power and responsibility from LEAs to schools for some aspects of the management of the teaching force. This is most evident in the area of in-service training. Here the recent introduction of Grant Related In-Service Training (GRIST) requires LEAs to provide each school with the resources to meet staff development needs as identified at school level. This may enable schools to provide support and follow-up which can be related to the outcomes of staff appraisal.

Schools have approached staff appraisal from at least three different positions. Perhaps the school self-evaluation initiatives were the least threatening and most distantly related to the direct processes of staff appraisal. Elliot (1981) points out that by 1980 two-thirds of LEAs in England and Wales had been involved in discussions about school self-evaluation and many had already produced guidelines indicating to schools how they should go about evaluating themselves. Clift (1982) suggests that some of the self-evaluation schemes which followed these guidelines concentrated on asking about institutional procedures while giving scant attention to the outcomes of learning and making virtually no reference to standards (e.g. ILEA, 1977). The use of these schemes tended to be left to the individual schools. At the other extreme Clift identified a small group of schemes, exemplified by that of the Oxfordshire LEA, which contained the external validation and moderation of internally assessed standards. This scheme was mandatory in Oxfordshire schools. Clift argues that all LEA school self-evaluation schemes were expected to promote professional and institutional development, as well as rendering the schools in some way accountable for what they were doing. He suggests that self-evaluation may lead to an awareness of institutional or professional shortcomings which is necessary before remedial action can be taken. Such an awareness, while being necessary for remedial action, is not sufficient of itself to ensure that remedial action is taken. He concluded that school self-evaluation will not produce institutional or professional improvements without a massive input of managerial and leadership skills and without some means of ensuring that teachers become involved in those activities which might produce such improvements.

Perhaps as a result of reaching conclusions similar to those above; perhaps out of a recognition that the introduction of teacher appraisal would become almost inevitable; and perhaps out of a desire to establish and own an appraisal system appropriate to their own schools, a number of LEAs have begun to establish staff appraisal procedures in schools. Some of these, such as the Suffolk scheme, are a product of DES pilot projects, while others are the result of initiatives from within the LEA itself. These schemes vary in a number of ways, not least in the extent to which they place the emphasis on the evaluation and development functions of the appraisal process. Sidewell (1987) has suggested that the Croydon scheme is one which places considerable emphasis on evaluation and accountability. It will

7

measure student performance against standardized tests. Staff appraisal will then be related to these results. This scheme is explicitly geared towards promotion within the LEA with potential candidates for promotion being selected for special training. In the newly revised Solihull scheme, however, the developmental and evaluative functions are given equal emphasis:

Purposes
1. Evaluation must be seen as ongoing and applicable to all levels of the service. Its purpose is to provide information about the service in order to improve the quality of the service and to demonstrate accountability.
2. To encourage personal and professional fulfilment and development of staff.
    (Solihull, 1986, p.7.)

Staff appraisal here is seen as an integral part of the overall process of school evaluation with the intention of supporting and developing effective practices and of generating programmes for action. The responsibility for this remains with the school, unlike the Nottinghamshire Professional Development Programme, in which much of this responsibility rests with the LEA's Inspectors (Nottinghamshire, 1985) and where appraisal is part of a developmental structure. This emphasis is carried even further as part of Cumbria's approach. This scheme is specifically developmental in intent and has been established with teachers. It stresses the need for reaching an agreement over targets and criteria by negotiation and for Inspectors to carry out a professional development function (Cumbria, 1985).

As Nuttall (1986) has argued, therefore, there are a large number of appraisal schemes which have been devised by LEAs. Perhaps even more schemes have been devised by individual schools. James and Newman (1985) discuss a number of such schemes and suggest that, on the whole, they are essentially formative and developmental in nature and tend to ignore the summative aspects of teacher evaluation. The predominant model is one of an interview centred on target setting and on the evaluation of the extent to which targets set on previous occasions had been reached. This is linked with an identification of appropriate career development plans and necessary staff development training. Although schemes fostered by LEAs tend to combine both summative and formative aspects of appraisal, I.B. Butterworth (1985) has argued that some school schemes are based on departmental reviews which combine individual appraisal with a review of the curriculum and of organisational factors, although most of these schemes have not been in existence long enough for their effects to have been examined. (Turner and Clift, 1985.) Many of these schemes are given different titles. Some are described as 'staff appraisal' but many will be identified as 'career planning', 'career review', or 'personal professional development'. Some are even given a simple title of 'work review', 'person review' or simply 'review'. In essence however, it is the meaning attached to the scheme rather than the descriptive title given to it which is important. As I have argued elsewhere (Bell, 1987) it is possible to identify a range of meanings which have been or could be attached to different staff appraisal schemes. In the next section I wish to consider briefly some of the more common sets of meanings which have been attached to a variety of attempts to justify the introduction of staff appraisal into schools and colleges.

The meanings attached to staff appraisal

Teachers respond to the idea of staff appraisal in a number of different ways depending on how it is presented to them. As Arnold demonstrates in chapter five, to introduce staff appraisal into any school is to generate change. This process, like any other change, requires careful and sympathetic management in order to minimize the threat which it may be thought to contain by the staff of the school, and to reduce the potential for conflict. Several contributors, including A.J. Richardson (chapter seven), and S.M. Slater (chapter six), raise these issues. Teachers' attitudes towards staff appraisal are also determined, in part, by the meanings which they attach to it and by their interpretations of the meanings attached to appraisal by other significant people. This section will examine six such sets of meanings which have exerted a considerable influence over staff attitudes to appraisal processes in schools in recent years.

(i) *Identifying incompetent teachers*

The first and, perhaps the least positive and helpful rationale used to justify staff appraisal in schools was that based on the need to identify incompetent teachers. This position was predicated on the view that the teaching force needed to be

9

cleansed of teachers who were in some way incompetent and who were probably responsible for the ills of the education system. The most significant example of this position can be found in Sir Keith Joseph's speech at the North of England Education Conference in January 1984, in which he argued that it was vital for incompetent teachers in our schools to be identified and removed. He argued that there was a case for removing 'such teachers from a profession where they can do such disproportionate harm' (*TES*, 13.1.84). This view was tempered somewhat when he denied wishing to link annual appraisal to instant remedies or penalties, (*TES*, 22.11.85) though this did not mean that the idea would be dropped. He pressed this view further by asking students to comment on the comparative quality of the teachers during private meetings with them on several visits to schools over a 2-year period. This belief in the existence of a substantial number of incompetent teachers has proved difficult to sustain but, nevertheless, it is still implicit in a number of statements on appraisal contained in DES publications. In particular it can be found embodied in *Better Schools* (DES, 1985a) and in *Quality in Schools: Evaluation and Appraisal* (DES, 1985b). Furthermore, the insistence that: 'The employing authority can only be satisfied that each school is *properly staffed* if it knows enough about the skills and *competences* of individual teachers' (Joseph, 1985: my italics) served to reinforce the view that appraisal was, at least in part, about the analysis of competence and, therefore, the identification of incompetence.

To place emphasis on the identification of incompetent teachers when discussing the DES's position was, according to David Hancock, Permanent Secretary at the DES, to misconstrue the Department's intentions and motives (Hancock, 1985). It was not intended to use appraisal to remove unsuitable people from teaching although, 'Where the appraisal reveals unsatisfactory performance and it persists even after counselling, support and training, then action must be taken in the interests of the college or school and its students. In the last resort, staff whose performance cannot be restored to a satisfactory standard ought to be dismissed. The burden of an incompetence which has proved to be irremediable weighs heavily on *colleagues* – a point frequently overlooked.' (Hancock, 1985, pp.4–5.)

In spite of this, Hancock stressed that appraisal ought to be seen, not as a threat but as presenting a series of opportunities, not least of which might be to earn more money or gain promotion.

(ii) *Improving pay and promotion*

The linking of appraisal to pay and/or promotion should not be seen as payment by results (Hancock 1985). Rather this linking is an attempt to ensure that informed decisions are taken about the career progression of school teachers. In short, 'decisions directly affecting career development within the current salary structure – internal promotion and references for external promotions for example – should be as well informed as possible' (Hancock, 1985, p.5). This knowledge, he argued, can best be acquired through staff appraisals which focus on performance. In matters of performance, 'It remains the Department's view that a pay system which rewards exceptional performance in the classroom would be very much in the interests of the teaching profession and of the nation.' (Hancock, 1985, p.18.)

Joseph re-inforced this view when he argued that, 'During the period of continuing contraction that lies ahead, I believe that a solution is most likely to be found by way of reforms which link higher pay to high quality performance in the classroom and in the management of school.' (Joseph, 1985.)

In *Teaching Quality* (DES, 1983) we find a similar suggestion to the effect that appraisal could lead to the best teachers obtaining relatively greater rewards for their classroom expertise. In advance of the new *Pay and Conditions of Employment* (1987), Angela Rumbold, a junior minister at the DES, could be found suggesting that, 'you'd be pretty daft if you did not think that it's going to be linked ultimately. I think it will come slowly but surely.' (*TES*, 13.2.87.) 'It' in this context was the direct linking of pay and promotion to the appraisal of performance.

The process of assimilating teachers onto the new salary structure has been described by the National Union of Teachers (NUT) as the identification of the super teacher and is based on the assumption that better teachers deserve higher pay and that the appropriate process for identifying the high quality teachers is staff appraisal. This view has been supported by Trethowan (1985) who argued that the problem of how to motivate teachers can only be solved by rewarding the efficient and effective teachers more adequately. His main reservation is, however, that there will be insufficient money available for such a system and if funds are not provided then our schools will suffer. While it cannot be denied that there is a definite need for the present Burnham salary structure to be reviewed and replaced by something more appropriate to the last quarter of the twentieth century, it seems unlikely that the identification of appraisal as the process by which a restructuring might take place will do anything other than alienate teachers since it will be regarded by them as a punitive measure if it is related to salary and merit pay. The NUT makes this quite clear in *Teaching Quality* (1984) where it is argued that 'the union is opposed to assessment of teacher being linked directly to financial rewards' (p.48). Similarly, the Assistant Masters and Mistresses Association (AMMA) have taken a view that appears to try to reconcile two sets of meanings. They acknowledge that one purpose of appraisal is to aid planning for promotion (AMMA, 1985) and that appraisal will lose much of its credibility if its outcomes are not seen to be related to career development. Nevertheless, AMMA's document argues that linking appraisal directly with promotion and salary increases can only serve to inhibit the frank and honest discussion which is so necessary. A number of teachers' professional associations regard as equally inhibiting a view of appraisal which seeks to place the identification of incompetent teachers and the pay and promotions issue in the hands of groups external to the school.

(iii) *External accountability*

A set of meanings attached to appraisal and based on the view that there are a significant number of weak teachers who need to be removed from the system in order to restore public credibility in education has been developed by Eric Midwinter. He justifies his support for teacher appraisal by arguing that 'surrogate consumers', that is parents, should have more say in teacher appraisal. This would, he argues, allay their anxiety about, 'bullies, mental now more than physical' and the 'no hopers and nincompoops' as well as the 'idlers' who now teach in schools and who were recruited during the late 1950s and early 1960s when it is argued standards of entry were dropped at a time of acute shortage. Midwinter places considerable faith in the power of parents to assess who the 'good' and 'bad' teachers are. He goes on to argue that 'the lore of the launderette is unerringly accurate' (*TES*, 8.2.85) and that to involve parents, and members of the wider community outside schools would improve teacher credibility among the public. In a similar vein, Kenneth Baker has argued that it is no longer possible to continue with a system of education under which teachers decide what pupils should learn without reference to clear nationally agreed objectives, and without having to expose and, if necessary, justify their decisions to parents, employers and the public (*TES*, 16.1.87). The new curriculum responsibilities which are devolved to school governors, while not directly involving them in staff appraisal, do give them significantly more influence over the school curriculum should they decide to exercise it. Thus teachers must be accountable and must be seen to be accountable.

This set of meanings, like the first two, are based on a 'deficit' view of schools and the teachers who work in them. The three sets of meanings share the view that there is considerable room for improvement within the teaching profession. The point of departure is over how such an improvement might be best brought about. The search for the incompetent teachers as envisaged by the DES would be carried out according to the criteria set out in DES publications and would presumably inform those staff appraisal procedures which LEAs would establish. From Midwinter's perspective appraisal would be carried out by groups of parents acting, presumably, as vigilante representatives of all of the parents to a particular school. Quite how this process would work is never spelled out. Whatever the outcome of such a process it is doubtful whether it would lead to anything much more than plugging gaps in provision, while it would probably serve to demoralise the conscientious rather than to motivate or improve the incompetent. It is highly unlikely to lead to any real improvement in performance, however this may be measured.

(iv) *Improving teacher performance*

Strangely enough, a similar set of meanings to those outlined directly above, and containing an implicitly 'deficit' model of teachers, is evident when the views expressed by headteachers and LEA representatives are considered although, in this case, incompetence is replaced by demoralization, and the appraisal process would be carried out by teachers themselves within their own schools. The use of staff appraisal for motivational purposes is well documented in industrial circles. The extent to which this deliberate provision of a Hawthorn Effect will work is not clear, but the assumption that it will is certainly built into a number of management courses, and has also been made by HMI who argue that in many cases appraisal procedures, 'lead to a better working climate and to improved performance by the schools and by individual teachers' (DES, 1985b, paragraph 141).

This emphasis on improving teacher performance can also be found in *Better Schools* (DES, 1985a) where it is argued that all teachers need help in assessing their own professional performance and in building on their strengths and working to improve their limitations. To that end, systematic nationwide arrangements for appraising teacher performance are essential. How far such appraisal needs to be based on classroom visiting and upon an appraisal of both pupils' work and of the teacher's contribution to the life of the school, as suggested in *Teaching Quality* (DES, 1983) is open to doubt. Certainly, from this perspective,

> The Cornerstone of appraisal schemes is the belief that teachers wish to improve their performance in order to enhance the education of pupils. Following from this is the assumption that appraisal systems should have a positive orientation: that is, the purpose of appraisal should be to develop teachers professionally rather than to "get at" them . . .
>
> (Suffolk LEA, 1985. quoted in *Evaluation and Education*, joint issues 9/10 April, 1986, p.10.)

However, as Wilcox (1986) has pointed out, the observation of performance – particularly if attempted on some kind of systematic basis – would appear to distinguish teacher appraisal from many of the appraisal systems which operate in industry, commerce and the other public services. These typically consist of a structured interview reviewing past progress and agreeing to future targets. They rarely include pre-arranged and systematic observation of people's day-to-day performance. This difference seems to have gone by unremarked in the current debate. We, however, examine in detail in chapter nine the planning and preparation necessary for classroom observation as well as, in chapter three, that necessary for structured interviewing. As will be shown in several chapters, especially six, seven, and eight, the appraisal process can generate significant amounts of valuable educational information about the staff of schools. This, in itself, provides a fifth rationale for appraisal. Such knowledge, it is argued, can contribute to the more effective management of the teaching force.

(v)   *Effective management of teachers*

If the set of meanings which links motivation, reward and appraisal is perceived as hostile and threatening by teachers and their representatives then the argument that appraisal might be justified in terms of the needs which schools and LEAs have to plan the staffing in educational institutions could, at first sight, be regarded as more neutral. Again, Sir Keith Joseph has argued (1985) that LEAs need to know about the skills and competences of individual teachers and that such knowledge can only come from some form of systematic appraisal. This view was recently re-asserted in *'Those having torches . . . '* (Suffolk LEA, 1985) which drew attention to the need LEAs have for more information upon which to base their planning as well as the need for resources to establish schemes of staff appraisal and to train relevant staff.

Hancock, quoting a DES policy statement on this subject to be found in *Teaching Quality*, stated that:

> The Government welcome recent moves towards self-assessment by schools and teachers, and believe these should help to improve school standards and curricula. But employers can manage their teacher force effectively only if they have accurate knowledge of each teacher's performance. The Government believe that for this purpose *formal assessment of teacher performance is necessary.*
> (Hancock 1985, p.2.)

Furthermore, he suggested that this need for information on which to base management policy was not confined to the LEAs. Managers in schools also: 'need accurate and up-to-date information on performance in post in order to take good management decisions – for example, about staff deployment and in-service training.' (Hancock 1985, p.5.)

This view, especially in relation to the LEAs, is developed further in *Better Schools* (DES, 1985a) where it is argued that regular and formal appraisal of the performance of all teachers is necessary if local education authorities are to have the reliable, comprehensive and up-to-date information to facilitate effective professional support and development and to deploy teachers to the best advantage. In the light of statements such as these, it is quite understandable if teachers in some circumstances regard appraisal as an attempt to introduce, redefine, or reinforce redeployment practices, especially in those schools which are beset by a significant problem of contraction in pupil numbers, rather than as a process in which professional development has a central place.

(vi) *Professional development*

Perhaps the least threatening of all the inherent sets of meanings as far as teachers are concerned is that which links staff appraisal to the professional development of teachers. This view emerges both in the documents produced by LEAs such as Solihull and Cumbria, and also in some DES publications. In *Teaching Quality* (DES, 1983) it was argued that those managing the school teacher force have a clear responsibility to establish a policy for staff development and training, based on a systematic assessment of every teacher's performance. Staff appraisal schemes which are geared primarily to identifying in-service needs, or other kinds of experience that might enhance career development, appear to be, at least in part, acceptable to many teachers if the views expressed in the publication of teacher unions is to be accepted. The NUT (1984) argues that what is required is an annual dialogue or career review between the teacher and a more experienced colleague, within which the emphasis would be on planning the teacher's professional development, evolving improved or more appropriate teaching skills, and upon supporting teachers rather than placing them in a competitive situation for promotion. This, it is argued, would increase job satisfaction and would benefit the school as the needs of both teachers and schools could be analysed and identified. With this in mind, the NUT would support a regular staff review since, it argues, all staff would benefit from regular periods of discussion and evaluation with a senior member of staff or headteacher or, with the agreement of the teacher concerned, with a member of the authority's advisory staff, about their current work and possible in-service education needs (NUT, 1984). AMMA's view is even more positively based on the view put forward by Hancock (1985) that formal appraisal may be the only opportunity for giving praise where it is due.

Montgomery develops this point further when she points out that: 'The essence of appraisal should be positive. Appraisal should be about "prizing" and "valuing" what is seen.' (Montgomery 1985, p.16.) Even Sir Keith Joseph recognized that an appraisal system is also needed for the professional enhancement of the individual teacher (Joseph, 1985) while Hancock linked appraisal with its outcomes. 'To be fully effective an appraisal system would have to be complemented by better arrangements for the individual teacher's career development – including induction, in-service training, guidance on possible teaching posts and promotion.' (Hancock, 1985, p.3.) This view is also stated in *Teaching Quality* (DES, 1983) which stresses the need for the provision of professional development and support for teachers. It is made clear both here and in *Better Schools* (DES, 1985a) that those managing the teacher force have a responsibility to establish a policy for training based on an assessment of every teacher's performance.

Thus it appears that a range of meanings can be and, in practice, often are attached to staff appraisal by those most affected by it, that is the teachers. As a result of their interpretations of what appraisal means, teachers' responses may vary from outright opposition and rejection to a position in which the fundamental questions are how staff should be appraised and what the likely outcomes of the process are. As Wilcox (1986) suggests, therefore, appraisal is neither a simple nor a unitary concept. Teachers' responses to it will depend upon their perceptions of its purposes and, in particular, whether it is formative or summative.

Perceptions and responses

Responses to appraisal at the individual, institutional and the professional association level are, it has been argued above, mediated through sets of meanings which are attached to the process. Opposition to appraisal will almost certainly be generated by the summative elements of appraisal. These summative elements may include establishing direct accountabilities, determining pay levels or promotion prospects and improving performance. The more formative aspects will be related to the extent to which the process is used to provide a context for career and professional development and to situations where specific outcomes of a developmental nature can be identified. Thus, if appraisal is to be part of a set of strategies by which teachers are to be held accountable, then this accountability must have a developmental emphasis and be a process of professional accounting to colleagues within the education service.

In fact, a small survey of teachers interested in staff appraisal indicated that the major difficulty associated with the introduction of staff appraisal tended to focus on the natural suspicion that many teachers have of such a change in their working conditions (Bell, 1985). This suspicion was manifested in two forms. Firstly, it focused on staff appraisal which could be regarded by teachers as a direct attack on their own professional autonomy. Teachers have, in the past, exercised this autonomy within their classrooms almost to the exclusion of all other forms of influence. A staff appraisal process which impinged on the right of teachers solely and entirely to make professional judgements about activities within the confines of the classroom would threaten that jealously guarded privilege. Secondly, suspicion was also expressed by some teachers about the ability of their colleagues in middle or senior management to carry out an effective appraisal process or to implement such a process impartially because of past problems or past professional relationship difficulties. These two basic suspicions lead to a natural reluctance to accept this change.

Another difficulty which many teachers identified was the extent to which they would be placing themselves in a highly vulnerable position if a staff appraisal process required them to indicate those areas in their professional life where they were experiencing problems or were requiring help or further training; it was felt that such information might prejudice promotion prospects or lead to a general diminution of their esteem without their school. It was also argued that staff appraisal, if carried out badly, would increase the level of cynicism within the schools and lead to a lowering of teacher morale. There would be a lack of commitment not only to staff appraisal, if this were to happen, but this lack of commitment might also spread to other areas in which change was desirable. The major barrier to implementing staff appraisal effectively was believed to be the extent to which those training needs or staff development needs, which were identified by the process, could or would be met by the school or the LEA. Clearly, in order to overcome the suspicions and concerns, any staff appraisal process needs to be introduced into a school carefully and effectively. This means that all those to be involved in such a process require training before the system can be introduced, and the extent to which such training is required and the time that it would take was also identified as a difficulty with introducing an appraisal system. Concern was expressed about the extent to which LEAs and schools could provide the necessary training, and the extent to which those people who were to be in the position of carrying out appraisals would recognize that such training was necessary.

In spite of those very real fears, anxieties and reservations Hancock, speaking in 1985, clearly indicated that the Secretary of State would seek powers to enable him to make regulations:

> . . . requiring local authorities to appraise their teachers with a certain prescribed minimum frequency and laying down a national framework for the way in which appraisal might be done. We recognise that it is entirely possible that everything needed to create a national appraisal system will be settled in negotiations between the teacher unions and the employers and that every authority will agree to operate in broadly the same way. But it is also possible that the outcome will in practice be a great deal more untidy than that. I can envisage circumstances in which it would be generally agreed that the education service as a whole would benefit from regulations prescribing a framework for an appraisal system to cover teachers in all colleges and schools.
> (Hancock, 1985, p.11.)

As was shown above, this has now happened. Small wonder, therefore, that a significant number of LEAs and a rapidly growing number of schools have responded to this situation by devising their own staff appraisal system. This book used the experience of some of those schools as a basis for a practical guide to colleagues in all types of schools who may soon wish to develop an appraisal system for their own school. In chapter two Norman Thomas discusses some basic principles and raises some broad questions which must be considered when contemplating the introduction of staff appraisal to a school. Kingsley Bungard, in chapter three, provides a detailed, planned approach to appraisal in which staff in schools can devise an appraisal system to suit their own particular situation. This framework was applied by C.D.M. Rhodes to his own school, and he describes the process in chapter four. An alternative approach to the introduction of staff appraisal is analysed by Francis Arnold in chapter five. Here a consultant used a similar process in three schools with some interestingly different outcomes. From these experiences a series of stages through which the introduction of staff appraisal might pass are identified, together with a suggested time scale. In chapter six S.M. Slater shows how the introduction of staff appraisal to two schools has led him to believe that the process must be directly linked to a discussion of aims and objectives for all the school as well as of its consituent parts. A.J. Richardson, in chapter seven, develops a similar theme when he considers staff appraisal in his primary school. He locates its introduction in the context of a series of wider discussions about the professional concerns of the staff in his school and about possible ways of further developing the existing expertise of his classroom-based teachers. The professional development theme is picked up again by Jenny Morris in chapter eight. She shows how she was able to use a voluntary appraisal process to help to facilitate the amalgamation of three schools by linking a staff development programme to the needs identified by the process. The process was, itself, a significant factor in helping to create a sense of identity for the new school. The headteacher was not directly involved in this process but the relationship of the headteacher to the appraisal process, and the vexed question of who appraises the headteacher is considered by Harry Moore in chapter nine where he sets out to deal with the issues raised for the head by staff appraisal. Another contentious issue, the role of classroom observation in staff appraisal, is discussed by Clive Carthew in chapter ten. He provides some guidelines for those who wish to include appraisal in the classroom as part of their staff appraisal process. The final chapter will consider the main advantages and disadvantages of staff appraisal and will suggest that, if it is to be successful and acceptable, it needs to be an integral part of the school's staff development programme.

Chapter 2

The Appraisal of Teachers

Norman Thomas

Informal appraisal

As we saw in chapter one, appraisal has always been part of daily life in all schools. Teachers appraise children, sometimes to elucidate where a child stands as compared with others, but more often to judge what he or she knows and can do so that decisions may be taken on what to move on to next. For the most part covertly, children form views about each other and about their teachers, and teachers form views about each other. The appraisal that has been most influential on practice has arisen from teachers' personal reflections on their own work.

Teachers' opinions of each other have in the main been arrived at informally and incidentally. They are shaped, as it were, out of the corner of the eye or from what is discovered about what children know when taking over responsibility for their teaching. There have been two main circumstances in which the process has been more formal: teachers in their probationary year have had reports written on them and forwarded to the LEA; and heads have written accounts of teachers' work and effectiveness in references and testimonials when new jobs or promotions are sought. What is now being proposed, and what we expect to be generally established, is a systematic and overt appraisal of the work of teachers. That process is the subject of the rest of this chapter.

Norman Thomas

The purposes of formal appraisal

A formal appraisal system should serve one principal and two main dependent purposes. The principal aim should be the improvement of children's education, and the worth of any system should be judged by the nature of the improvement it produces.

The first dependent purpose is the professional development of the teacher. The appraisal process should enable a teacher to become increasingly effective in his or her current role; it should make possible adjustment to the present role that would make better use of his or her strengths; and should open up the possibilities of major changes of role, either within the school or elsewhere, so that the teacher may make progress in the profession. The second dependent purpose is the management of teachers within the system. At school level this can help to determine what new role a teacher might best undertake to forward the work of the school as a whole. From a broader viewpoint, it might lead to the identification and development of the next generation of heads; or ensure that the system responds to children with special educational needs by identifying teachers with marked sympathies for children in difficulties; or stimulate movement between schools so as to make better use of a teacher's talents where numbers are falling in one place and growing in another, or where there is some specific shortage of interest and expertise. It follows that a satisfactory appraisal system is not simply a process by which teachers are assessed. It must include the means by which the implications of assessments are put into effect, taking account of the principal and the dependent purposes.

The criteria used in appraisal

The first stage in the appraisal process is to define a teacher's job. There is, at the time of writing, no generally agreed definition available, and though current national discussions on conditions of service may provide general headings, more detail is required for day-to-day practice. It would be a mistake to conceive of an appraisal system as applying to unchanged arrangements and unchanging requirements upon teachers. Any appraisal must take account of the school environment, the size and nature of its catchment area, and any changes that are taking place inside the school – whether by intention or force of circumstance – or in its surroundings. Anyone who must later take account of the results of an appraisal needs to have regard to its context as well as to its specific result.

Given that there are differences of role within schools, differences between schools, and changes over time, how far is it possible for assessments to be expressed in general terms valid in all primary teaching? Is it enough to assess broadly whether the teacher's work is sufficiently prepared, appropriate to the children and followed up, that order is maintained, that reasonable relations are established with other members of staff and with parents, that the teaching area is kept in a satisfactory condition? The difficulty with such broad headings is that superficially similar assessments may mean different things for different teachers and in different schools. The appraisal may require the use of specific criteria, depending on the nature of the teacher's job within the school: differentiating levels of work between three or four children in a remedial group does not present the same problems as differentiating between 35 of a wide age range in a mixed catchment area; the elements of differentiation best used in teaching a group of 3-year-olds are not the same as for a class of 11-year-olds. In one school, 'order' may be judged by whether the children are quiet and deferential; in another, it may be thought right for children to be inquisitive, questioning, even of the teacher, and buzzing. Establishing satisfactory relations with other members of staff has different connotations in a school where teachers work largely separately as compared with another where each acts as a coordinator in some aspect of the curriculum. Furthermore, if a teacher knows only the broad headings used for assessment he or she would have to guess at the appraiser's preferences within headings. A similar difficulty would be faced by anyone who was later required to interpret the result of the appraisal.

Within schools there should be a sharper definition of the teacher's role – the job description – than can be provided by broad headings alone, and the definition should be negotiated with the teacher before an appraisal period begins, and certainly on taking up a new job. Negotiation with an individual teacher should be conducted within the context of the general practices and policy of the school. The statements on these and the job descriptions of individual teachers should be formally adopted by the governing body. They should be sufficiently detailed to enable individuals within the school and outsiders to comprehend the principles on which the school works, and the direction in which it is moving, and they should allow the teacher and others to know the basis on which appraisal is conducted. They should be reviewed at appropriate intervals and especially in connection with the appraisal of the head, whose responsibility it is to see that they ·are implemented. The wider ground on which the school definitions are based should be provided by the LEA which, in its turn, should draw on a broader, national agreement. If the area and national definitions were closely defined they would be too limiting on a school.

A system of appraisal must make allowances for differences of practice between one appraiser and another by the inclusion of moderating procedures. There are three main kinds of difference that need to be minimized. One leads an appraiser to judge everyone to be a swan – or a goose. A second arises from bias with regard to individuals. A third stems from differences in the criteria used or variations in the emphasis placed upon them. None can be wholly eliminated and so caution is needed in using an appraisal system as operated at school level in deciding, without additional checks, whether a teacher is or is not, for example, fit to remain in teaching, or to be offered a headship. The appraisal system may usefully provide some evidence towards making such decisions, but it has to be remembered that a teacher who is regarded as ineffective in one school may be more effective in another, and the management aspect of an appraisal system would be met in part if teachers were enabled to transfer to schools in which their talents would be better used.

These considerations strengthen the notion that one should regard the appraisal system as being concerned with the relationship between the teacher and the job, and with improving that relationship, and not as being directed towards grading teachers against each other. Of course there are extreme cases of people who are not suited to being teachers, but these should always be few given the arrangements for entry to the profession. Some teachers may have become unsuited due to ill health or difficulties in their lives outside school. Whatever the case, their problems should have been identified and dealt with before a routine appraisal system runs its course, even if it is operated yearly or biennially.

It is assumed that apposite judgements can be made about teachers' abilities to lead children to behave in ways regarded as desirable, to enthuse them, and to provide suitable levels and kinds of work. These all have relevance to the principal purpose of appraisal: to improve the education of the children. Can anything more specific be included? There are considerable doubts about the wisdom of giving prominence to the bald results of tests on the children and even of assessments of their work, whether done by teachers or others, unless account is taken of the circumstances in which the work is done and the ways it changes over time. Children who, in an absolute sense, are achieving well for their age may owe proportionately less to the school and their teacher than other children whose achievements are modest or even poor as compared with those of the population as a whole, as is well known. Yet, plainly, there is a need to take account of children's achievements and progress. A wholly satisfactory way of determining the 'value-added' benefit that children get from attending school is not known, but for further development the work done in connection with the ILEA 'Junior School Project' (ILEA, 1986) is commended, in the hope that some such measure might be *part* of the evidence used in considering a teacher's work.

Methods of appraisal

No formal system will entirely displace informal methods of appraisal. Much of the evidence for the formal system will be collected informally, but the formal collection of evidence should not take place only near to the end of an appraisal period. One cycle in the procedure should include more or less continuous informal assessment, with discussion in its course, and a number of more formal occasions, prepared for and sometimes requested by the appraised. We regard observation of teaching as essential. Experiments should be carried out to discover what part different methods of observation might play; the appraiser and appraised working alongside each other; the appraiser as a neutral observer; the use of video recording; the use of observation schedules; the examination of children's written work; the appraiser taking on the teaching role; discussion with the appraised of the appraiser's notes or completed checklist. Some possible approaches to classroom observation are discussed in chapter ten.

Plainly, classroom observation is not enough if aspects of the teacher's work outside the classroom are not to be included. The appraiser needs to have sight of the teacher's working notebooks; to have some means of judging the appraised's relations with colleagues and others who work with or for the children, such as the educational psychologist or health visitor; and with the children's parents.

The formal interview and the written report

A formal interview towards the end of an appraisal cycle is a necessary part of the process. It is part of the preparation of the formal written statement, not the occasion for its transmission. There does not seem to be a single best form. A variety of forms should be tried out, and it may always be desirable to permit some variations, even within one LEA; some suggestions are made in chapter three. Any written report should be seen by the appraised who should be able to add his or her own comment. It may be necessary for the management of the system that the written report, or more usually part of it, be sent elsewhere but this should not be an automatic part of the procedure. It should happen when the action called for by the appraisal is beyond the control of the appraiser and appraised, for example where one or preferably both parties take the view that attendance at a specific course, secondment or promotion is necessary, or possibly in the course of moderating the system. There may also be cases where the appraised may wish to call in evidence what has been written about effectiveness in previous posts. We stress again that all arrangements for appraisal should be developmental in form, allowing for and recording change in the individual and in the school, and that appraisal which compares the performance of real teachers to that of an ideal teacher is likely to be unprofitable.

Who should be appraised?

If any teachers are appraised, all should be, including deputies and heads. Of course, there are some practical difficulties, especially for teachers who work on supply, but we believe that they should be included. Arrangement should be made to appraise all who conduct appraisals, including LEA advisers who do so.

Who should appraise?

There is some indication from Dr Clift's work at the Open University that many teachers prefer assessment to be conducted by the head. They see the head as the person who knows the context and the school climate, who could take managerial action as a result of the assessment, and who would be influential in any applications they made for posts outside or inside the school. In secondary schools, particularly, they saw the head as more detached than, say, the head of department. At least one of the teachers' associations, the NUT, takes a different view. It stresses the part that the appraisal process will play in professional development rather than its part in managing the system, and argues for appraisal by peers, with nothing being passed on except by agreement with the appraised. Another possibility is for appraisal to be carried out by senior members of staff other than the head. Still another is for the job to be done by LEA inspectors.

It is believed that the last proposition is impractical so far as the main body of teachers is concerned, especially given the need for appraisal over a period. However, it is considered there are five important contributions that should be made by LEA advisory services. The first is in discussing with the school the direction that it should be taking, bearing in mind the limits of the LEA's resources. The second is to arbitrate where there is disagreement between appraised and appraiser (whether or not the head is the appraiser). The third is in appraising heads. The fourth is in providing some moderating influence between schools. The fifth is in the training of appraisers and appraised. These demands will put great strain on the LEA advisory services as they are now constituted, and especially so with regard to primary schools, which account for something like four fifths of all heads. The idea that ex-heads should appraise heads is noted but not enthusiastically received. Whoever does the job should have the right of continuous access to the school and be conscious of recent pressures and developments, which not many retired people can be.

It is not easy to see that someone other than the head can act as the main appraiser in primary schools (with the possible exception of the relatively few large schools with 20 or more teachers) if the senior/junior relationship between appraiser and appraised is adopted. Increasingly, it is unrealistic to expect a head to have superior expertise in every aspect of the curriculum, one or more of which may be important in relation to an individual teacher, but appraisal is concerned with teachers' ability to carry and develop specific roles and with their needs for wider professional development. The primary school head remains the person best placed to make a general appraisal of this kind. In secondary schools it may be that deputy heads and even heads of department have a role in the appraisal process.

It has been considered whether appraisal might best be between peers including, possibly, peers from different schools. Such arrangements, by themselves, would not satisfy all three purposes of appraisal as here defined, and especially that relating to the management of the system. Nevertheless, it would be worth experimenting with appraisal by a combination of head/ peer action, especially where the peer is from a different school. By the same argument, the appraisal of heads might be undertaken jointly by another head and the LEA inspector.

There is clearly room for experiment in ways of combining the roles of the two contributors and obvious issues are: who should take the lead, the peer or the superior; should both appraisers always/ever draw on the same evidence; how should the peer be selected, e.g. by the appraised or by the senior appraiser, or by a third party to supplement the curricular expertise of the head; should all discussion be between the three; to what extent should the appraisers reach and record their conclusions independently; should there be one final statement with room for dissension? The key factor is that those being appraised should be regarded as having a positive part to play in the appraisal process. The appraised should also have the right to require specific evidence to be examined. Indeed, in advance of the main appraisal interview it is desirable that the appraised should provide a written statement outlining the main tasks performed over the period of the appraisal, the appraised's own view of his or her performance, and his or her main aims and training needs for the period ahead.

The resource consequences of an appraisal system

There is no escaping the fact that any appraisal system worth the name requires resources. Of course, some will come from a more pointed use of activities that are already being undertaken. But it is not possible to do everything necessary by a simple rearrangement of existing work. The first additional requirement is time (and expenses where external appraisers are used) for the appraisers to carry out the formal aspects of their work, not least the recording of observations and discussions. The second, though it may turn out to be the largest, is time for the appraised which might require his or her temporary replacement by a supply teacher. Appraisal is likely to create large demands for in-service support, not merely for attending a course but also for visiting other schools and other classes in the appraised's own school, and for bringing in specialist advisory help. The link between appraisal and in-service training will be strengthened by the operation of Section 50 in the *Education Act, 1986*. A third demand may be for material resources necessary to carry out the teaching ideas that arise from appraisal. Special attention must be given to the needs of small schools where the head has a substantial teaching programme, and where there are few teachers to provide expertise across the curriculum; various arrangements that are being adopted in clustering small schools, or small schools with larger schools, may have their advantages in this connection also. In all kinds of school, time will be required for establishing a tighter definition of intentions and priorities.

Unless sufficient resources are available to undertake appraisal properly, including training appraisers and enacting the necessary consequences of appraisal, any attempt to introduce a system will lead to frustration. Without adequate resourcing it would be better not to start. We are aware that 'sufficient' and 'adequate' are relative terms, not absolutes. The volume of resources needs to be such that teachers see that appraisal will work in a positive way to improve their effectiveness as teachers. The imposition of a system unacceptable to teachers would damage education. If, however, teachers can see that the schooling will be helped to become more effective, and that their worth will be better recognized, then the system of appraisal may be a tool for improvement, and have an uplifting effect upon the climate and quality of education in all our schools.

Postscript

Since the 1987 General Election there is the promise of a substantial Education Bill and some indication of policy matters that may be included within the Bill. Some of these, depending on the precise form of their enactment, will have consequences for the appraisal of teachers. Assuming that a national curriculum is formulated and put into operation, it seems inevitable that the requirements of the curriculum and teachers' response to them must be taken into account in any appraisal system. Exactly how will remain obscure until the nature of the curriculum is settled.

At the minimum, one must assume that teachers will be expected to include in their teaching whatever is contained within the curriculum and be appraised on the extent to which they do. Nothing that has been said to date leads one to suppose that every detail of the curriculum will be laid down: some reports have suggested that the national curriculum will be required to occupy a proportion of the time available, leaving more to be done outside it; even in the time that it does occupy, one hopes and supposes that the detailed subject matter to be studied by children will be relevant to their lives and locality, and that there will be the possibility of differentiation between children according to their aptitudes, abilities and interests; though perhaps within some defined parameters. The process of appraisal, if these suppositions are realized, cannot simply be mechanical, but must depend on some judgement as to whether the teacher's interpretation of the national curriculum is appropriate. The establishment of the curriculum will provide a comparative against which to judge the teacher's performance, though it will not make the judgement simple.

But it is not yet possible to envisage what the curriculum will contain. It could be that some fairly crude subject headings – English, mathematics, science, etc. – will provide a structure. Or it would be possible to use a different framework: to say what skills, ideas, attitudes it should foster, and which broad topics should be studied. It might in either case indicate the changes that should occur as children mature. The second approach was taken in the DES policy statement, Science 5–16, and would present one kind of appraisal problem.

Alternatively, the national curriculum might lay out, in as far as it can be done, some important pathways of learning, marking critical stages, so that children's progress can be plotted and recorded – by means that are for discussion elsewhere. The question is then raised whether children's recorded progress with a teacher can form part of the evidence to be taken into account when appraisal is undertaken. There are some unresolved difficulties that should be borne in mind. Some come from the backgrounds of the children (whether they should or not): disharmonies of attitudes and approach between home and school prevent some children from making the progress that others do; children who come into school with little or no English, or pronounced dialects, may take longer to get going than others accustomed to the school's form of English. All of the factors that influence children's absolute levels of achievement, no matter how defined, and including hereditary as well as social factors, also influence the rates of children's progress. The appraiser cannot apply simple mechanical rules either about levels of achievement or progress and suppose that justice will certainly be done in the appraisal. Interpretation and judgement will still be required.

An advantage that may come, if the national curriculum is well devised, is that teachers and appraisers will be aware of some of the evidence to be taken into account in the appraisal; the purposes will be clearer. A danger is that the teacher will be tempted, from a sense of self-protection, to force-feed children so that they can regurgitate but have not digested and cannot use what they are taught. We cannot yet know whether the advantage will be realized. We can, I think, be satisfied that people will still have to interpret the evidence about teachers' performance, and that it will take time, experience and compassion – for the teacher as well as for the children.

Notes

An excellent *Appraisal: Annotated Bibliography No. 1*, compiled by B.S. Niblett, is available from the National Development Centre for School Management Training Resource Bank, NDC, 35 Berkeley Square, Bristol, BS8 1JA.

This chapter was originally produced as a paper as a result of discussion in the Primary Education Study Group.

An earlier version of this chapter was published in *Education*, 28 August 1987. We are grateful to the editor of *Education* for his permission to publish the material contained in that article.

Chapter 3

A Planned Approach to Staff Appraisal in Schools

Kingsley Bungard

What is appraisal?

Appraisal is a professional system of two-way communication between a head of school or a head of department and an individual member of staff. It is a positive means of helping a manager of staff to develop the potential of his or her teaching and non-teaching colleagues. In order to maintain a positive approach the manager concentrates on performance aspects and seeks to help the appraisee assess:

* How well he or she is performing.
* Whether he or she can improve in any area of their work.
* The actions to improve the appraisee's performance.

Other issues can be covered in addition to present performance and these are likely to be the appraisee's ambitions and aspirations – his or her potential for taking on more demanding jobs. Actions to be taken to develop new skills, as well as views and feelings about the department or school, can also prove to be useful areas to explore. It is worth pointing out at the beginning the range of issues to be covered. Care should be taken to avoid discussion of personal qualities which cannot be rectified. Appraisal is entirely performance related, leaving the appraisee with a clear understanding of how he or she is getting on, and reaching an agreement with the appraiser about the ways and means of improving performance where necessary.

Appraisal, if regarded in this way, is a powerful motivational technique. It provides genuine recognition – which all individuals in the teaching profession need.

The advantages of effective appraisal

Before discussing a system which can be used in schools it is worth examining the potential advantages of investing time in introducing appraisal.

Potential advantages for the individual:

- He or she knows where they stand regarding their own performance.
- He or she knows where they are going in terms of improvement and development plans.
- He or she gains a greater sense of belonging through realizing the value of their contribution to the school.

Potential advantages for the appraisee and the school:

- A better understanding of how staff see their jobs and how satisfied they are.
- The opportunity to plan for improvements in performance.
- The opportunity to plan the best use of ability and potential.
- An insight into the effectiveness of one's own management style.

It may be thought that all this can be achieved through daily contact with staff. Such a judgement would be misleading. The real benefit of a planned and practical approach to appraisal is seizing the opportunity to stand back and take stock.

A planned approach

In the next chapter an experienced headteacher will describe the way in which an appraisal system was introduced into his school. This chapter makes the assumption that the introduction of appraisal has been successful. Three stages will be explained:

Method of preparing:
- Deciding what should be covered in terms of structure and content of interview.

- Preparing for the interview and helping the member of staff prepare.

Conducting the interview:

- How to carry out a thorough interview concentrating on the performance and improvement needs of staff.

- A description will be given on the use of interview skills to ensure the member of staff makes the major contribution to the interview.

Follow-up:

- Examining the technique of recording actions for improvement or development of the member of staff.

- Methods of putting action plans into practice.

If the appraisal system is to be truly professional, all three of the stages outlined above need to be taken seriously. Appraisal is not just about conducting a good interview, that is only one third of the process. Both preparation and follow-up are an integral part of the planned approach. Entering into the appraisal arena with anything less than a 100 per cent commitment and conviction will lead to failure. Appraisal is an extremely time consuming exercise and will bring a huge investment for the future. However, it could also bring the uncommitted headteacher and the system of appraisal into disrepute.

Preparing for appraisal

There are two aspects to preparation for appraisal.

The first is the appraisee's preparation, including organizational arrangements, as well as deep consideration of the appraisee's performance.

The second aspect of appraisal is helping the appraisee to prepare in a constructive and positive manner that ensures the interview is performance related. This section sets out to describe what must be completed by both parties before the appraisal interview.

Preparation for the appraisal

Firstly, decide a standard structure and content for all appraisal interviews. It is very important for staff to recognize that everyone is treated in the same manner. Failure to observe this simple rule could result in insecurity of staff, who may be left wondering why they were asked different questions or, worse still, why certain questions were not asked! So prepare a standard set of questions for your appraisal. Listed below is a suggested sequence of questions.

• What are the most important areas of the job?
• What are his or her strengths – the things he or she has done well?
• What are the main problems he or she has encountered?
• Can these problems be avoided in future?
• What are his or her staff training and development needs?
• What is the best way to achieve each improvement?

The above points deal with performance in his or her present job. If you want to cover future opportunities as well, these are possible further interview points:

• What abilities, if any, are not being fully used in his or her present job?
• What new jobs could he or she take on in the coming year?
• Does he or she want to take on more demanding jobs?
• What is the best way to develop each new skill?

Finally, if you also want to check job satisfaction during the interview, include points like the following:

• What aspects of the job give him or her most satisfaction?
• What things, if any, cause dissatisfaction?

Secondly, it is essential to make detailed arrangements to ensure the degree of professionalism does not go by unnoticed in the eyes of school staff. It is therefore recommended that you carry out the following procedures.

• Set a date, time and place for appraisal interviews. The beginning of the summer term has a lot of advantages, but care should be taken to avoid appraisals drifting into the last two to three weeks of the summer term. Written notices, along with public announcements of the precise times, reduces the risk of people forgetting the appointment. Be mindful of risks, if you

choose your office or study. If there is no option, what arrangements can be made to avoid interruptions from the telephone or people knocking on your door?
- Give at least two week's notice of the interview to each member of staff.
- Brief him or her on how to prepare. The following six questions should be set out on paper equally spaced to allow for written responses:

1. *Performance*: Consider your performance since the last appraisal and comment on your most important achievements. Itemize particular results and successes which you influenced.
2. Consider your performance since the last appraisal – comment on your disappointments with respect to your own responsibilities.
3. *Obstacles*: What factors outside your control hindered you in achieving a better performance?
4. *Training and new experiences last year*:
   (a) What training or new planned experiences did you undergo last year?
   (b) In what ways have they helped?
5. *Increased skill or knowledge*: What part of your present job could benefit if you received additional training or new planned experiences?
6. *List of training needs*: As a result of completing the whole form, list the areas of training or planned experiences you need in order to further develop your professional expertise.

It is important to explain to each member of staff the value of giving time to complete this document. Draw attention to the fact that it is confidential and a copy of the responses need to be returned at least two days before the interview. This gives the appraiser the opportunity to consider the appraisee's points of view.

The appraiser's preparation

Before the interview, go through each of the questions asked of the appraisee. Try to recall the key areas of performance from your point of view. Very often the member of staff misses some key areas of their year's work, especially those which have been successful. This is one opportunity to ensure you take complete stock of each person's performance. The focus for appraisal is improvement of performance and development needs. It is therefore important to concentrate on these issues and not the negative aspects of a member of staff's contribution to the school. For example, there is little value in telling staff about their poor attitude, lack of enthusiasm and cooperation. It is far better to get their agreement to achieving specified results, in a given time. This is far more positive and provides a better basis for appraisal the following year, when agreed targets from the year before can be analysed. Only then can comments on enthusiasm, and attitude be pointed out as a contributing factor to their success or failure to reach targets.

Provisionally, in the appraiser's preparation, decide any realistic improvement or development aims. These targets may not be the finally agreed targets, but may well be in the areas that you feel are important to the school. Typical target areas to be considered are listed as follows:

- New projects, e.g. refurbishment of library,
                      introduction of computers,
                      new procedures for sports day.
                      new form of record keeping.
- Change of teaching post in the school.
- Developing a new system for timetabling.
- New curriculum initiatives.
- Examination results or test performances.

Setting targets is a skill which will not be dealt with in this chapter. Suffice to say, make them measurable, and put deadlines on the completion or achievement of the target. For example, to ensure that the library is re-arranged as discussed with heads of departments, the project is set to be completed by the end of spring term.

The final part of your preparation is to try and anticipate any problems that might arise during the interview. For example, if there is very severe criticism of school procedures. Or equally as challenging, if there is a lack of recognition that a job has been carried out well. The message here is to plan beforehand how you are going to handle them.

In summary, there are four areas on which the appraiser should concentrate before the interview:

- Read carefully through the appraisee's responses and decide the areas you agree with or where there are gaps.

- Concentrate on things that have gone well and improvement needs.
- Think of realistic improvement or development targets for next year.
- Think about ways in which you could help or support the member of staff to achieve their targets.

Asking your member of staff to prepare is an important stage in appraisal. You are seeking to gain commitment, so that you both treat the appraisal as a genuine opportunity for improvement. Share the initiative with your staff.

Conducting the interview

It has already been said that it is worth making a conscious decision to use a room where the risk of disturbance is low. It also important to consider the arrangement of the seating. Use upright chairs and a table where both people can sit together. Although the appraisal interview should be conducted informally, it must still be business-like. Relaxing in comfortable chairs with a coffee table between you is unlikely to produce the sense of importance and urgency of the situation. Finally, as a prelude to the conduct of the interview, leave 2 to 3 minutes to have your paperwork ready, the table and chairs in the right position, so that you are ready to welcome your member of staff to this important event.

The sequence of the interview is based on two clear principles. Firstly, ask the appraisee to comment on each issue, then comment in response and add to the points raised. Secondly, move from strength to weaknesses and finish on actions to improve or develop. This allows the interview to end on a positive note. The following is a suggested structure:
Leave 2–3 minutes to look through your notes.

Approximate timing

1. Outline the interview plan. — 1 minute
2. Ask appraisee to describe his or her strengths – things achieved. — 7 minutes
3. Acknowledge good work and contribution to the school. — 7 minutes
4. Ask appraisee what problems/obstacles have made his/her job more difficult. — 7 minutes

5.	Agree ways to eliminate problems/obstacles.	7 minutes
6.	Ask what aspects of work need improving.	7 minutes
7.	Tell staff what aspects of their work need improving.	5 minutes
8.	Agree improvement aims for the coming years.	10 minutes
9.	Jointly decide actions needed to achieve improvement aims.	10 minutes
		60 minutes

Leave 5 minutes before seeing anyone else to ensure you have noted the agreements or actions. During the interview the appraiser's interview skills are of paramount importance. The following are designed to be hints and tips to ensure the appraiser conducts a professional appraisal interview.

Interviewing skills

There are four basic skills in conducting an appraisal interview:

Establishing trust.
Listening accurately.
Reflecting feelings.
Questioning.

Establishing trust

A person will only talk to you frankly about his or her improvements if he or she wants to. The following are aimed at helping your own attitude during the interview or discussion, to encourage him or her to open up by establishing trust:

- Take a genuine interest in the other person.
- Show concern to have issues resolved and agreements reached.
- Try to understand, and accept his or her views and feelings.
- Don't criticize, or try to put him or her down.
- Don't pressurize him or her or force the pace.

Kingsley Bungard

Listening

'Being a good listener' is a real skill. It is more than being silent – you have to show, in the way that you listen, that you understand what the other person says, without necessarily expressing agreement or disagreement. Listening well requires that you:

- Don't interrupt. Let the other person do the talking.
- Concentrate and hear what he or she says (rather than what you want to hear).
- Assess the underlying feelings, behind what he or she actually says. (How does he feel about it? Does he feel strongly about it? Does he really mean what he is saying?)
- Look at him or her while he or she is speaking. This shows that you are listening.
- Encourage him or her to carry on talking if you want further explanation. You can do this with very few words – a nod, a noise of agreement, or a short phrase like 'Why?' or 'Tell me more'.
- Don't rush in to fill pauses and be patient.

Reflecting feelings

The good appraiser acts as a 'mirror' to help the other person to stand back and examine the improvements critically and calmly. At intervals during the interview it is a good idea to state the feeling and meaning behind what is being said to you rather than the facts themselves. These are ways to do it, to keep the interview moving positively:

- Summarize feelings and meanings in your own words, as statements rather than questions.
- Reflect his or her actual feelings. Don't try to lead or interpret.
- Keep it brief, reflecting the last feelings expressed, not the whole interview.
- Don't try to catch out the other person or pin him or her down by referring to inconsistencies or apparent inaccuracies.
- Reflect constructive ideas or decisions only when the other person is calm and confident enough to act on them. Initially you are acting as a safety valve, to let the other person give vent to feelings.

Questioning

If the other person is not very forthcoming you can ask questions, to start him or her talking. The types of question you ask are important – they must encourage him or her to open up, but they must not be threatening in any way. Follow these suggestions:

- Ask open questions that require explanatory answers.
- Avoid closed questions that require yes or no answers only. The affect may be to close the issue down rather than open it up.
- Use general 'encouraging' statements or questions ('Tell me more', 'Can you add to that?', 'Can you give me an example?').
- Avoid questions that imply criticisms or set a trap.
- Avoid forcing questions that push the other person towards a decision or action.

In summary, the appraiser is attempting to achieve maximum participation. Here are seven points to adhere to:

1. Work through your interview plan in sequence and note conclusions or agreements reached between you and your member of staff.
2. Begin each interview stage by asking the views of your member of staff. Only come in with your views afterwards – to add to what has been said or introduce a forgotten point.
3. At the start of the interview, concentrate on important areas of the job and the teacher's strengths. Readily acknowledge good work achieved – it is important to show that you appreciate the value of their contribution. Deal with improvement needs only after you have covered strengths.
4. Give the teacher the opportunity to identify improvement needs before giving your own views.
5. If the member of staff has a real weakness and improvement needs and fails to identify them, do not hesitate to say what they are, firmly and clearly. But make the criticism clear and crisp – moving quickly on to ways in which improvement can be achieved through positive action.
6. Do not be afraid to recognize criticism of yourself or the school. Quickly turn to ways of avoiding such points arising again.
7. End the interview on a strong positive note, agreeing clear improvement or development aims for the months ahead and

actions to achieve the aims. Above all, try to achieve maximum participation.

Using this approach to conducting the interview makes note-taking very much easier. Instead of several pages of essay style manuscript an action plan is really all that is necessary.

List of actions	to be completed by

This approach to note-taking should be open-style, either photocopied or written out by the appraisee, so that both the appraisee and appraiser have copies. There is no point in making comments about a person if they themselves have not seen what has been written. Equally, it is important to write the comments in action terms, focusing on what is to be done to remedy the situation or to develop new skills. Note-taking in this format makes follow-up so much easier, because appraisal does not end with the interview.

Follow-up

Formal appraisal should take place once a year. The agreed actions noted down from the previous year will be a useful basis for preparation and the initial review of the year's performance in next year's appraisal interview. However, it is too long to wait for many of the likely actions agreed between the head and the member of staff. The appraiser has a managerial responsibility to help staff satisfy the needs and check whether the agreements reached at the appraisal interview have been carried out. When dates have been put down against actions it makes the follow-up so much easier. Providing the head has noted the dates in his own diary, brief follow-up meetings are so much easier to handle.

There are three possible levels of action you may decide to take in order to improve or develop a member of staff's needs.

Briefing

For the simplest needs it may be enough to explain and discuss what he or she should do to improve. But even with the simple needs, follow up to check that he or she has taken the necessary action. For example, if a teacher is often late in doing the register, you may simply emphasize the importance of getting it done on time, and direct him or her to take immediate steps to improve.

Coaching

More complex needs are best handled by coaching. Decide the aim and draw up an action plan – things he or she can do, and ways you can help, to achieve the aim. If the plan is going to take some time, decide time targets against each action. Follow up to check progress against the plan. For example, a young teacher is weak at preparing her work priorities and using her time effectively. You can draw up an action plan:

- Ask her to keep an activity log for a week (recording her lesson plans).
- Analyse the log entries with her, examining how she did her planning.
- Ask her to prepare a simple daily plan each day.
- Review what she does against her plan, initially on a daily basis.
- Continue to review her use of time at less frequent intervals.

Formal training

If a member of staff has to overcome a major weakness, or if you want her to prepare for a job that is entirely new to her, it may be best if she attends an outside course. Do not assume that this will, in itself, satisfy the need. Follow up, to help her apply what she has learned in her job. For example, if you want to develop a member of staff to take on a staff development role, you may decide to send her on an appropriate course. This would be a first step in learning and applying managerial skills.

In this chapter the author has described a practical and planned model for those who wish to introduce appraisal to their school. The approach is based on practical experience. In the next chapter a headteacher describes how he interpreted this approach in practice and introduces some ideas that will help to ensure the planned approach to appraisal really works.

Chapter 4

Practical Appraisal in Primary Schools

C.D.M. Rhodes

Introduction

An examination of the introduction of an appraisal system into my school must be seen against the background of the nature of the school itself, the self-appraisal and review strategies which already existed, and my management training.

The events to be described took place in the summer of 1985. At that time the school was a three-form entry 8–12 middle school, serving the south eastern corner of a small Midlands town. Work was class based, with subject coordinators time-tabled to permit some cooperative teaching. Non-class based staff were responsible for French, Music and CDT. Science was taught by those with a particular interest in the subject. Additional staffing was deployed to support those children whose first language was other than English, and provision was made for pupils with special educational needs. Twenty teachers worked in the school, five of whom were part time.

A university based management course led me to see appraisal as a positive and valuable way in which to enhance the professional development strategies already employed in the school. I saw appraisal as a professionally structured process through which teacher and head could review the former's work together, and plan for an effective future. It was to be an opportunity for both to take stock, for praise to be given, and plans made in order to support any aspect of the teacher's work which might need to be enhanced. It would provide a regular opportunity to review the effectiveness of in-service work and to establish priorities for the future. This chapter will discuss a pilot scheme run in the school in order to test the appraisal methodology suggested on the management course.

Self-appraisal through 'forecast' review

The staff were already used to a form of self-appraisal. At the beginning of each term every member of staff is asked to prepare a forecast of the work they hope to cover during the term, and the organizational strategies they intend to employ in order to achieve them. As an example, a third-year teacher might write as follows about the Maths work she hoped to achieve with her children:

'All the class will be working from the Scottish Primary Maths Group materials.

'Alan and Mary should finish Stage 4 by half term, and will be put onto problem solving cards. At the moment they are using the DART computer program, and are learning how to draw various designs on the computer using different programming techniques.

'The other Stage 4 group are working well and should finish the book next term. I take each topic and work the group together on that for approximately two weeks.

'The first Stage 3 group should have completed this book by half term, and will then start on Stage 4. There should be no problems here.

'The second Stage 3 group. A very slow working group of 5 children all with difficulties in most topics . . . ' etc., etc.

Staff would submit these forecasts by the end of the second week of term. The forecast forms the basis of a discussion with me, and any revisions would be agreed by both the teacher and myself. The agreed alterations were usually of a minor nature. In the example given above, the revision might see a more specific reference to the actual materials the first group are going to use, a comment on marking strategies, or detail about the organization of practical activities.

The final version was then typed up by the school secretary, and one copy returned to the teacher as the agreed organizational and curriculum targets for the term.

Teachers undertaking extra responsibilities, either voluntarily, or as part of a scale post, were asked to submit their 'post' aims in a similar manner.

The postholder for AVA, for example, might write: 'As agreed, I will be continuing to order and collate the teacher's notes for the TV programmes we use. I hope that Mrs Chalmers, our new classroom helper, will be able to relieve me of the task of making the daily video recordings. She has a video of her own and . . . I am looking forward to the course on video cameras,

45

and hope to borrow one after half term. I would like to run a film making club, and will be working with Dawn who wants to make a permanent record of the school concert. I will be running a mini-course for staff on use of the heat copier for the next three hymn practices . . . '

Two weeks before the end of term, a copy of the forecast is returned to the teacher. This is used as a 'scribble' document, and is annotated by the class teacher in the light of what really happened. This self-appraisal is very useful in that it allows the class teacher to make a professional review of the past term. Successes can be recorded, alterations dictated by expediency can be noted, disappointments mentioned. The exercise is professional and non-threatening. It serves as the start point for an informal review of the term with the headteacher. Praise can be given, and professional discussion can take place about how the work has gone. Their joint conclusions and comments provide the basis for the following term's forecast, and give indications for future in-service work.

Typical comments made about language work might read: 'Writing – story book for younger children. This project is not finished but should have been completed early next term. I am pleased with the way the children have made genuine efforts to find out which type of story six-year-olds enjoy and have thought very carefully about vocabulary and presentation . . . I have continued with the weekly spelling lists. For all their faults, they seem a relatively painless way of dealing with phonic and spelling rules, vocabulary etc . . . I was not at all happy about the decision to change our policy on library books. I realize that I was in a minority at the staff meeting, but I would like an opportunity to raise the subject again. I would like to chat to you informally about this . . . '

The following term's forecast would follow naturally on the previous one. In consequence, the actual amount of revision at the beginning of each term was usually small, if necessary at all. End of term reviews, however, were usually very detailed and the basis for fruitful professional discussion. Hence it can be seen that even before the launch of the appraisal project, there was a solid foundation of professional mutual review.

Self-appraisal by the children

The older children, too, were being introduced to the idea of self-appraisal. It is my custom to sit down with each individual child, hopefully once a term, to hear them read, and talk through their work and progress. This takes place within the classroom during normal lessons. I have a simple form of record card for each child. The older children are encouraged to self-evaluate their work and progress, and agree the comments to be put on the card. Targets can be set to be met by the next review. I found the children to be very honest in their self-evaluation. It is interesting to note that the better children tended to be self-depreciating, and that most would start the self-evaluating process by using criteria or standards which they thought I would require rather than their own. Therefore, the most common start point would be a comment about neatness, or when asked to choose a piece of work of which they were really proud, they would choose a page of ticks. I therefore need to probe a little more to indicate what I really wanted and establish criteria.

Sometimes the classteacher would sit in on the review, and this was even more productive. I do not think that the children have felt over-powered. We usually sit three to the table, with the classwork and record card before us. A three-way discussion takes place, with references back to previous comments on the card and to the children's own work. I also use this card as a basis for discussion with parents, and am perfectly happy to let them read the comments on it. You can see from the children's faces that they are concerned about what is written about them, and some ask what happens to the card. There is a sense of professional acceptance when they have agreed to the comment, even if it is critical, so long as it is fair, and support strategies have been discussed for the future. There are some important lessons for adult appraisal here, too.

There is no doubt that the exercise requires a lot of time, but I am convinced of its value. It is obviously valuable to the children themselves, who now enjoy the process and enter into the discussions positively. Clearly, the younger children need guidance as the process will be very new to them. It also gives me an invaluable strategy whereby I can be in classrooms naturally for long periods without the teachers feeling uneasy. It gives both myself and the classteacher opportunities to discuss individual children and share pleasure over progress, disappointment over under-achievement or concern over disadvantage.

C.D.M. Rhodes

The concept of formal appraisal

To sum up the situation at Easter 1985:

(a) The staff were used to the concept of self-appraisal, and professional development based on past experience and existing practice is well established.

(b) Staff were used to seeing the headteacher in the working classroom, evaluating and discussing work with the children, and afterwards with the teacher. Implicit in this is an informal but structured evaluation of the teacher's work with that group of children.

In April 1985 I was seconded as Course Tutor on a 20-day DES funded management course for experienced headteachers of primary schools. It was based in a university department of education. The lecturers came from education, industry and from the university department itself. Course members came from five LEAs. One of the main elements in the course was an examination of 'management processes'. This was led by a management consultant with a wide experience of both educational and industrial/commercial management practice. Staff appraisal was one of his topics, and the day we spent examining the issues involved, he gave me considerable food for thought. I saw that the model he was suggesting would be a natural extension to the work I was already undertaking in school, albeit in a more structured and formalized way.

Understandably, my staff were expecting me to bring ideas back from the course, and I decided that formal appraisal might be a suitable topic.

I started by examining the actual agenda for the appraisal interview. Readers will recall from the previous chapter in this book that the interview is formed around responses made to a number of previously agreed questions. I decided to modify those suggested on the course so that they read as follows:

(a) Consider your work during this school year, and comment on your most important achievements. Itemize any particular results and successes you have influenced.

(b) Consider your work during this school year. Comment on your disappointments with respect to your own responsibilities.

(c) What factors outside your control hindered your achieving a better performance?

48

(d) What in-service training have you received during the past twelve months? In what way has it helped?

(e) What part of your present job could benefit if you received additional training?

My next step was to discuss the whole concept of appraisal, and the proposed questions, with my deputy, and the representative of the professional association to which the majority of the staff belonged. The latter was also the teacher-governor. He did not see any problems. Although this was a time of industrial action, the staff had already requested a full staff meeting to discuss some urgent issues, and it was agreed that appraisal be included on the agenda.

I had decided on one major change from the model suggested on the course. The lecturer had suggested that once the project had been discussed and agreed at the launch staff meeting, then copies should be distributed with sufficient space between questions to allow staff room to write their responses. The papers would then be returned to the head several days before the appraisal interview. This would allow the head to have time to consider the teacher's points before their meeting. I understood the logic of this arrangement, but felt that the process might seem too formal or threatening, and therefore better omitted at this stage.

Experience was to show that there were indeed points raised which I was not expecting. Foreknowledge of these would have been both to my advantage, and to the teacher's, as I would have had time to prepare my thoughts on the issue concerned. With hindsight, I would suggest that the matter is aired at the initial staff meeting, and a consensus position reached. As agreed, I raised the whole issue of appraisal at the staff meeting, and outlined the thinking behind the project. I circulated the questions, and asked for volunteers to carry out a pilot scheme. I stressed the theme of professional development, that it was a review and a look forward, and was totally unconnected with salary. During the ensuing discussion, it became clear that several colleagues did indeed find the concept threatening, and inevitably linked it with a national programme of monitoring. Others supported the idea, and argued that it was better to test and refine one's own scheme, than have an unsatisfactory one imposed by an external body.

Two weeks passed, and we were within a fortnight of the end of the summer term. No-one had come forward for the pilot scheme. A little alarming. Then the colleague who had already discussed the project with me in his capacity as union representative, came forward as the first volunteer. In order to hold the interview under the best possible conditions, I arranged for his class to be covered by another teacher. It was clearly important to place a high status on the discussion, and to hold it in the best possible circumstances. Trying to cram a professional dialogue into lunchtime when one might be interrupted, or after school when both parties were tired, would be clearly unproductive.

This does raise serious resource implications. I was able to arrange cover among colleagues for the pilot scheme, but this should not be the regular pattern. Most primary schools just do not have 'floating' teachers, and even if they do, they were appointed for tasks other than covering for appraisal interviews. However, on this occasion, the necessary cover arrangements had been agreed with staff, and I was able to fix the first appointment for eleven o'clock, after morning break, and requested that my secretary kept callers and interruptions at bay.

The framework for the appraisal interview

The actual setting, too, required careful planning. Primary headteachers' rooms or offices are usually small, and only permit a limited number of permutations of furniture. Several basic principles obviously apply when deciding the setting for the appraisal interview. It should be non-threatening, yet professional. Informal, yet businesslike. The traditional large desk, defended by its battlements of telephone, pen stand and in-trays, can be very defensive, especially if the visitor is expected to sit on the other side, and on a lower chair! The opposite scenario of two easy chairs can also present problems if the meeting is going to require writing and on looking at a number of sheets of paper. You could finish up with complete informality – on your knees, side by side on the floor.

My own room permits two seating situations. In the first 'working' position, the desk is against the wall, and I sit across a corner to my visitor. Both of us have a clear space for papers. The second position is the informal easy chair solution, with a coffee table in between. I seldom offer refreshment on these occasions, because one's first question always seems to coincide with the visitor's first sip, and he is placed in the embarrassing position of deciding either to abandon the drink in order to answer, or keep you waiting. Confident guests use the pause for tea as a thinking strategy.

I decided to hold the appraisal interviews in the informal setting, but suggested to the staff that they bring their notes and something firm to write on. This proved to be a perfectly satisfactory arrangement. Having agreed an agenda of six question areas, as detailed earlier in the chapter, and determined time and situation, the scene was set for the first appraisal interview. The content of that interview, and those that followed, must, of course, remain confidential to those who took part. However, some general organizational points can be mentioned and reference made to a hypothetical appraisal interview.

The average length of an interview or discussion was 40 minutes. I have already indicated the implications this has for the staffing resource in a school. There is a clear need for appraisal schemes to be backed financially, in order to fund supply staff to cover colleagues involved in the appraisal process. During my pilot scheme I was able to conduct seven appraisal interviews during the space of ten working days. This presented considerable organizational difficulties in terms of staffing and time, but I was, and am, convinced that if appraisal is to be seen as a part of a teacher's professional development, it must be conducted and resourced in a professional manner.

It became very clear during the interviews that the discussion had benefitted from careful preparation on both sides. All my colleagues had thought carefully about their responses to the questions. Many chose to work quite closely from notes. Several had discussed their responses with colleagues or members of their families. It was clear, too, that despite the informal termly discussions described earlier in the chapter, colleagues welcomed the chance to have a formal opportunity to discuss and review their work in the school.

It was also clear that it was important to have some form of agreed note of what had been decided during the interview. It is all too easy to leave a meeting with an incorrect impression of what has been decided. An appraisal interview needs to be minuted by the headteacher as he or she proceeds. For example, he might say: 'I'll make a note of that. We agree that you need more support for the slow learning children in your class . . . We agree that I will talk to the adviser to see if there is any chance of some in-service training in . . . We agree that you will . . . '

At the end of the interview the head must sum up the points agreed: 'Right, let's see what we've agreed. I will . . . You will

. . . Have I got it correct? Good, I'll get these notes typed up, and give you a copy.' The notes will, of course, be an important element in the next appraisal meeting. Were targets achieved, goals reached?

In practice, I found that the last two of my questions, those dealing with in-service training, needed far less time for discussion. The first three questions usually took half an hour to cover, and the last two, ten minutes between them. I already knew what courses staff had attended, and what they had thought about them. The real discussion was about future in-service work, both school based and county based.

The content of the appraisal interview

I have already stated that the detailed content of the interviews held in my school must remain confidential. However, some further general points can be made through the medium of extracts from an imaginary interview.

In this fictional interview, we meet Jaswinder Gill, aged 26. She has been a teacher at Rosemary Lane Primary School for two years, both of which she has spent in a cooperative teaching situation in the reception class. The other teacher in the team, Ann Butler, always takes the lead in decision making and planning. There are many Asian children in the school, and Jaswinder spends quite a lot of her time working with the children in her class whose understanding of English is limited.

HT: Come in Jaswinder, and sit over here . . . Is that all right for you?

JG: Yes, thank you.

(Getting the ice-breaker over efficiently, needs careful thought. You don't want to open up too wide a non-agenda subject. Time is too precious, and this is to be a professional interview.)

HT: I'd like to concentrate on the questions we discussed and agreed at the staff meeting. I'm pleased to see that you've brought your notes. I have too.

(It is important to say this. Jaswinder may need to be reassured that it is in order for her to refer to her notes during the course of the interview, and to know that you are prepared yourself, and will be using your notes.)

HT: Let's start by thinking back over the last twelve months. What particular successes have there been?

JG: I'm very pleased with the progress Amandeep's made. She knew very little English when she started school, and now she chatters away all the time . . . and I was also very pleased with the art work that came out of the visit to the fire station.

This was a suprise to the headteacher. He had not forgotten about the project, but had not thought it that good. It is important to pick this point up.)

HT: I remember that project. Tell me more about what pleased you.

(Just as there were things which Jaswinder had seen as successes but the head had not, so there were things he had seen during the year that were certainly worthy of mention, but Jaswinder had not seen them as being especially successful.)

HT: . . . and don't forget the work the children did in capacity. That produced some excellent results.

JG: Did you really think so?

HT: Certainly. The children were fascinated. Several parents commented on it to me. A great deal of excellent mathematical language was going on . . .

(It is important for the head to try and keep a strict timetable for the interview, otherwise later topics will become too rushed. If, after ten minutes, they are still on question one, he should seek to move things along.)

HT: Let's move on to the next question. Have there been any disappointments during the year?

JG: Not really, apart from the fact that I still don't have my own class. It's been two years now. It's not that I don't like Mrs Butler, I do, and I've learned a lot from her, but I do want my own class in September. I think that people see me as some sort of superior classroom helper. I'm not. I'm a fully qualified teacher, but – just because I can speak Panjabi, I have to stay . . .

(Most teachers have several key issues they want to make sure are raised during the interview. Jaswinder is determined to make her most important point now. The emotional temperature has gone

up. Her point is valid, but the head has had to deploy his staff in order to meet the needs of the children. He cannot ignore Jaswinder's plea, nor can he allow the interview to be side tracked too much from the agreed agenda.)

HT: I know how strongly you feel about this, and I do see your point, and I know Mrs Butler does too. Let me make a suggestion. I will ask the multi-cultural adviser if there is any way he can get some more funding to employ a part-time teacher to look after the E2L side of things. Talk it through with Mrs Butler, and write out a list of exactly what and when you have to work specifically with the non-English speaking children. If you can do that by the end of next week we can rough out some form of job description. Can you make 12.30 next Friday?

(It is important for the head to set an exact timetable, with deadlines, for both himself and Jaswinder. People work to deadlines. Vague statements about future actions tend to get lost.)

(The head must now get back to the agenda.)

HT: But thinking back over the past few months, were there any other matters? . . . We did discuss the behaviour problem you were having with Michael Jones. Have things improved at all? . . .

(The head will have failed professionally if he has waited until the appraisal interview before mentioning something in Jaswinder's work which he felt could be improved. There should have been discussion when the problem was first noticed. Now is the time to review progress.)

I'd like to mention pre-reading skills again. I still feel that you are . . . Did you see the notice about a course? . . .

(In-service comes later on the agenda, but it would be wrong to ignore this opportunity to suggest professional support.)

JG: Yes, I'd like that. I suppose if I really understood what I was trying to achieve . . .

(Time to move on in the agenda.)

HT: Now, were there any factors outside your control which stopped you achieving what you wanted?

JG: Yes. We could definitely do with some more large Lego. Is there any chance of any money?

HT: I think so . . .

(Later in the interview, the head sums up, and ends on a positive note)

HT: Before we finish, let me read over my notes. We've agreed to meet next Friday to discuss . . . We are going to check the courses on early reading skills . . . You are going to give me an order for . . .

Well, thank you very much, Jaswinder. I've enjoyed our talk. I feel that we have covered some very important points. And, well done again about Amandeep. You've done something very special for her.

The project reviewed

I have already indicated that the first interview in my own school was with the teacher-governor union representative. Shortly afterwards five other colleagues came forward to join the scheme, while others indicated that they would be happy to take part early in the following term. Two members of staff were due to complete a special one year project in the November, and suggested that this would be an appropriate time to review their work. I was very pleased with the ways the interviews went, especially when a colleague who had expressed reservations at the staff meeting came forward, and we both felt that the resultant interview was very productive.

During the summer holidays, external events overtook us. For reasons unconnected with our own pilot scheme, one of the main professional associations decided to ban all participation by its members in appraisal schemes being tried in the county. I could not proceed with some colleagues, and discontinue with others, and so I put our scheme into abeyance.

This was a useful period, as it allowed us time to reflect and refine what had already happened. Several colleagues from outside the school, for example, had raised the question of a moderator. A weakness of schemes like ours is the possibility of a personality clash, or difference of educational philosophy, between the participants, resulting in an unfair appraisal. If 'B' is appraising 'C', should not 'C' have the right of appeal to 'A'? And should not 'A' be overseeing 'B' anyway?

Who was to be the moderator for a primary school? The only

clear candidate would be the pastoral adviser, but however good that person may be, do they have the degree of knowledge of the personalities and internal dynamics of each of their schools to form a fair judgment? The only way such knowledge can be gained is by a series of extended visits to schools. This has resource implications, and threatens other aspects of their professional work. However, I understand that some counties are working in this way, and their results will be interesting to see. The adviser, presumably, would have a role to play in headteacher appraisal! A fascinating topic in its own right.

The major lessons learned

I had learned some important lessons during the pilot scheme:

1. The planning stage must involve the staff as a whole. Unless they see appraisal as professionally desirable, they will not support it, and it would be better to abandon the whole thing.

2. The questions, or agenda, for the appraisal interview, must be understood and accepted by all those taking part.

3. Careful preparation, by both parties, before the interview, is essential to its success.

4. The time allotted for the interview should be one hour, and guaranteed free from interruptions. It should be at a time of day when both parties feel fresh.

5. The interview should be conducted in an unthreatening atmosphere, be seen as a mutual review and planning session concerned with the professional development of the teacher concerned.

6. Appraisal needs adequate financial resources to provide supply cover for those taking part, and training for all those proposing to take part in appraisal schemes, before they are launched in individual schools.

7. Appraisal is unconnected with salary.

8. The appraisal interview should not be the first time that a teacher learns that the head feels they are under-performing, or that their work deserves special praise.

9. It must be done well, or not at all.

The way forward

In the two years since the events described in this chapter, appraisal schemes and the whole concept of appraisal, have been much in the educational news. The professional associations have been conscious of the need to protect their members from ill-conceived or inadequately resourced schemes. However, in several parts of the country, there have been significant moves towards agreeing professionally acceptable procedures.

I think that this enforced waiting period has been to the benefit of appraisal, especially when one sees it in its essential context of staff and school development. We have also seen the introduction of radically new ideas for school based in-service work. Two years ago, I would not have believed that we would come so soon to financially resourced whole-school INSET, or five INSET days a year as part of a teacher's contract.

The new opportunities for professional development afforded by whole-school INSET and contracted INSET days, means that staff have time to review and assess, not only the needs of the school, but of themselves as well.

It is here that appraisal will come properly into its own. Not as a strategy to tease out the weak and reward the good, not as an annual patronizing pat on the head or formalized mark out of ten, but as an integral part of the school's system of review and assessment of its performance. It will identify good practice, and methods of spreading that good practice wider. It will identify weaknesses, and link into the new opportunities for staff professional training and development in order to strengthen colleagues' work.

A good appraisal scheme will be one that is developed by the staff themselves, because they see it as an essential element in the development of the school. It will be non-threatening. It will be professionally organized and resourced. All the participants will be trained for appraisal, and will support its aims. It will afford opportunities of mutual review and team planning.

Finally, 'Appraisal' will lose its capital A in the minds of teachers, and be seen as just one of a number of professional strategies found in a school in order to enhance the teachers' work with their children.

Chapter 5

The Introduction of Staff Appraisal into Schools

Francis Arnold

'Let no man give advice to others, that has not first given good counsel to himself'

Seneca

'He that won't be counselled can't be helped'
Benjamin Franklin

Background

For a non-teacher, the opportunity of introducing change into schools is a rare one. During 1985/86 and January and February of this year (1987), I was privileged to work with three groups of teachers in developing appraisal processes for their respective schools. One was very conscious of the fact that the time of these activities was a difficult one for teachers. In 1985 and 1986 the dispute with Government was at its height, and there was still a patina of concern and resentment among teachers earlier this year which could colour receptivity and cooperation. With the very area of proposed change linking directly to some of the issues of the dispute, it was therefore heartening to receive such high levels of support and cooperation which produced workable and acceptable appraisal processes.

The background was research; it was – and still is – the writer's contention that appraisal should be seen as positive and forward-looking and that its benefits are far-reaching not only to the individual participant, but the organization. There was, however, a personal concern. With forty years' experience of appraising or being appraised, I wanted to see if military and industrial

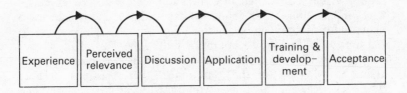

Figure 5.1   The training process

approaches were transferable. One accepted the need for adaptation in process but not in principle, and hoped that the benefits of appraisal would be accepted. This concern generated a question which had not been articulated and indeed had not even surfaced at the commencement of the research. There was a gradual awareness which developed into this query:

'Was one's commitment to appraisal based on many years' acceptance of a normative procedure which had proved successful, or was there a genuine personal belief in the principles of appraisal as being managerially, behaviourally and organizationally desirable?'

The question initially produced some uneasy responses. One of the problems of conviction, particularly when one attempts to persuade and influence through that conviction, is that it could be genuine belief, but it could also be the result of conditioning. The dilemma of faith against dogma is hardly new, but the analysis of purpose was useful and necessary, particularly where attempted persuasion is involved. It was important to ensure that one was not relying on techniques to attempt change. In the event, belief was found to be justified and the process fully transferable. Thanks to the receptivity of colleagues in Education, there was a reinforcement of conviction, but it is principally experience and application which will persuade Education to accept appraisal.

Experience of someone introducing, or assisting in introducing, appraisal, is significant and may be seen as a building-block for ultimate acceptance. Figure 5.1 shows how expertise and knowledge applied through training and practical application can effect change and acceptance. The process developed must also reflect that practicality of application and usage.

The context of hoping to introduce appraisal into the three schools concerned was the result, in each case, of a request. Two were large comprehensive schools and the third an all-girls' high school. Each had the benefit of a headteacher who saw appraisal as a fundamental responsibility of management, and as a positive change for improvement within their schools. There was no question of automatic acceptance by the school's staff however. The headteacher's receptivity and conviction did not necessarily reflect the views of the staff, and indeed there was no guarantee whatsoever that my invitation would lead to positive action. The headteachers perceived the value of using someone from outside their normal working environment, who could be seen as objective and independent, and as an agent for change. My task, therefore, embraced a need to gain approval and commitment through potential pilot groups to a process which might later be accepted by the complete staffs. For the two comprehensive schools, in 1985 and 1986, my role therefore was to be multi-faceted:

1. Persuader – of principle, need and benefit.
2. Developer – of process through involvement and shared ownership.
3. Facilitator – of actual introduction.
4. Analyser and evaluator – of the results with recommendations for action.
5. Provider – of training and development action to meet identified needs.

For the third school my role was to be ostensibly different but would embrace some of the above list. At the girls' school, I was to chair a working party which would represent all levels within the school. The need for the working party was accepted, and our purpose was to develop a tailor-made process for the school which we hoped would later be accepted by the remainder of the staff and subsequently be introduced. The role differences were subtle but nevertheless significant. For the two comprehensive schools, one was the supplicant armed with conviction but one hoped not zealotry. The process of acceptance necessitated initial acceptance of the actual need for appraisal, then a development of process with the consultant facilitating the activities through agreement but very much in a separate role as Figure 5.2 suggests.

Over a year later, in the girls' high school I was in many ways an

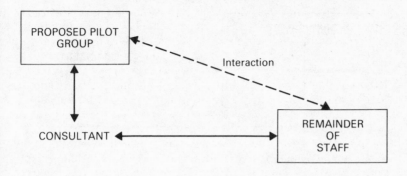

Figure 5.2   Generating acceptance

honorary member of staff as a fully fledged and accredited participant on the working party. The interaction here, shown in Figure 5.3, was distinctly different.

In our endeavours in the three schools, one was very conscious that appraisal should be seen as a means of motivational growth, and also as the Stewarts' (1977) 'moment of privilege'. It was not going to be particularly easy: the milieu (certainly during 1985) was not comfortable, but there was a shared desire for success. I will admit, at one stage, to thinking that what one was attempting was akin to one of Douglas Adams' (1982) character's suggestion that the knack of flying was throwing yourself at the ground and missing. Happily, we were able to develop more manageable approaches – albeit less spectacular.

Need for appraisal

Before examining the processes developed it was necessary to consider the reason for that development. Did the need for appraisal really exist (other than through some individual belief) in each school? The initial answer emerged as a qualified 'yes', providing certain safeguards could be built into the process.

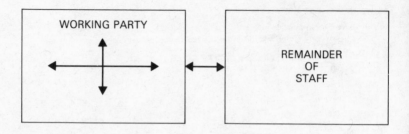

Figure 5.3 Interactions

These safeguards will be discussed later, but what was readily accepted was my own strongly-held views, (offered unashamedly and regularly to potential participants). These views were within the aegis of what I have somewhat grandiosely termed the *Four Laws of Appraisal* . . . .

1. Comment, appreciation, praise and criticism by one person of another must be made known to, and discussed with, that other person.
2. None of us should be expected to operate in a vacuum of assumption that there is an awareness, by others, of our needs, concerns, and aspirations.
3. That any appraisal process should be 'user friendly', and that it should not contain or generate any surprises, since appraisal had to be the formalization of an on-going system of continuous assessment and counselling.
4. That appraisal processes are only as effective and acceptable as those involved in them. This implies training, commitment, review and change.

There was a further view, more pragmatic perhaps, but it seemed relevant to the current climate of proposed change in Education: appraisal would come, there was every likelihood of its introduction. My contention was that the 'wise' school was one which anticipated change and developed an appraisal model which represented the individuality (in terms of ethos and environment) of the school. The alternative was to wait until some form of mandatory and unilateral introduction arrived –

with perhaps reduced opportunity for adaptation or flexibility to suit individual circumstances.

The references to change seem entirely appropriate. To introduce staff appraisal is to introduce a significant, and for some, worrying change. It is also a change process in its own right, since resistance has to be overcome, participation encouraged, and development effected with communication and purpose. Due to the general reaction to the very idea of staff appraisal one was acting as a change agent working with people, rather than as a change enforcer.

Killing and Fry (1986) categorize three change situations – anticipatory, reactive and crisis change. Their premise is that as change situations develop, the unsatisfactory management of one stage causes escalation to the next. My contention is that these models, as Figure 5.4 suggests, are entirely relevant to the introduction of appraisal. Without the acceptance of the need for the introduction of appraisal, effectiveness suffers, and in this context 'effectiveness' embraces motivation, well-being, competence and commitment. The longer it takes to introduce the change of appraisal – with the corresponding reduction of time for involving others in the process – the lower the level of performance.

My own work in introducing appraisal into the three schools would appear to fit into Killing and Fry's model. One was encouraging the concept of anticipatory change, with its opportunity of involvement and shared ownership, by developing change (appraisal) processes which are particular to each school. The pace of change here was through a series of incremental and gradual steps, with an emphasis on the need to reassure, to promote understanding, to focus on support and minimize delay or obstruction. The style of change introduction is participatory, with explanation and encouragement prevailing.

Missing this earlier opportunity could only lead to reactive change where the introduction of appraisal allows more limited time for that introduction and with the need to start to develop on a broader front. One could envisage the situation of schools being given a period of time in which an appraisal process had to be introduced. This would make the initial steps more hazardous in terms of resistance since the decrease in time would almost inevitably generate resentment and a lack of receptivity. Participation and involvement would be correspondingly diminished. The opportunity for school management teams to be proactive would be slight.

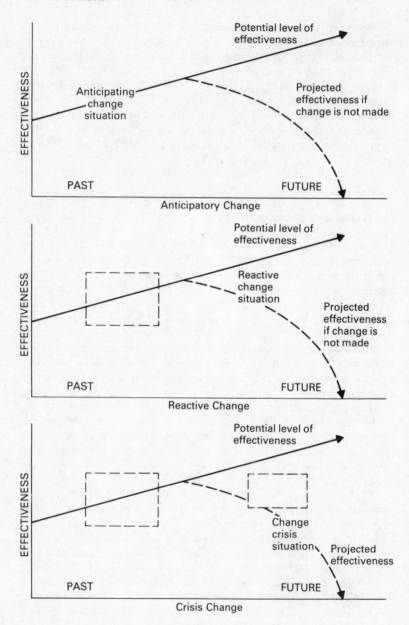

Figure 5.4   Three types of change

The third projection, of crisis change, suggests the mandatory introduction of staff appraisal with a need for fast, decisive action and a commensurate upheaval. Involvement would be limited to little more than reluctant acquiescence, but more seriously, any support (likely to be viewed as the result of unacceptable pressure) would be likely to be short-term only. With a risk of failure becoming increasingly higher through reactive and crisis change, it was apparent that my involvement in introducing staff appraisal could best be effected using an anticipatory change model.

Development of the appraisal process

Developing an appraisal process involves a series of linked stages which must be carefully and thoughtfully completed. For two of the three schools the process was identical, for the third there was one significant addition and several minor amendments. Examples of the actual processes will be given later in this chapter, but at this point, I shall provide details of the ones developed and employed, together with an indication of the time required for the various stages. The accompanying comments are in no way intended as definitive. Rather, they are observations against events with all the expected revelations engendered by hindsight. There were lessons learned with each exercise and, as often happens, the confidence suggested by an experience proved to be a motivating factor for commitment. Figure 5.5 shows the development process in overall detail and subsequent tables provide information and comment against each stage.

Situation analysis: (Stage 1)

The theme of this stage of the process is to analyse the situation (in this context the possible introduction of staff appraisal) with a view to identifying areas of concern and to obtain agreement to their resolution. As Stage One shows, areas of concern embraced the very concept of introducing appraisal, the roles of the participants, and the likely implications of that introduction. Agreement is clearly a need for advancement to subsequent stages.

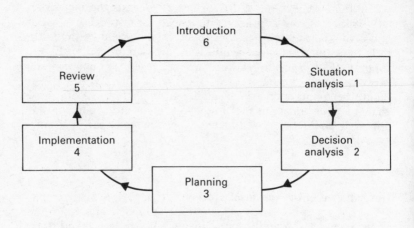

Figure 5.5 Introducing appraisal – the developmental process

Activity	Comment
Expression of concern	For all three schools the likelihood of appraisal being introduced as a facet of the professional teacher's working life was accepted. There was, certainly in individual minds, a feeling of inevitability, that there would be mandatory (and possibly, unilateral) introduction by central Government. The need for appraisal as a vehicle for development, and as a safeguard in terms of reporting and evaluation, was seen. Concerns centred around the question of confidentiality of the results (of an appraisal exercise), and the use to which those results might be put.

The role of the participants was clarified, resulting in the writer being accepted as: |

Activity	Comment
	1. A process consultant, who would initiate, advise and monitor the development of the process, and to whom the members of the pilot group would respond, with the possibility of negotiation and change (Schools A and B).
	2. The chairman of the working party where agreement had to be achieved within each working stage, thus obviating delay through proposal and response (School C, the High School).
Agreement	In Schools A and B this was given, but after a period of reflection and consideration by the potential pilot group. For School B this agreement was concomitant with my developing a 'reverse process' where the head of faculty would be reviewed by the faculty members.
	In School C agreement had already been determined prior to my assuming the role of chairman of the working party. Here, we obtained agreement to the principle of self-appraisal, plus the necessity for taking into account the complexity of reporting relationships.
Definition of the aim and objectives of each appraisal exercise	This activity is absolutely essential before further activities can be undertaken. There must be no question of developing a process first *then* deciding an aim which in some way matches that process. For Schools A and B, I determined the aim and objectives, offered these and obtained acceptance. They were:

67

Activity	Comment

Aim
To promote the most effective use of the human resource within the school, by reviewing Job Performance, Needs, Training, Development and Concerns.
Objectives
1. To develop an appraisal/review process which meets the determined aim.

2. To establish, by success through a pilot group, the credibility of a review process which could encourage other members of staff to participate.

3. To generate improved communication links between staff and headteacher.

School C

Aim   To promote professional development by identifying individual and group strengths and needs in order to improve overall performance and increase our ability to respond to further opportunities.
Objectives
1. To identify and agree for the coming review period individual and group roles and objectives.

2. To establish a participative and viable review process which will enable us to identify and provide response to, and support for, agreed training and development needs which will be communicated throughout the school.

Activity	Comment
	3. To show awareness and appreciation of identified strengths and contributions.
	The aims and objectives, once defined were displayed in the staff room with a request for the immediate communication (to any of the working party) of any concerns or objections; none were received.

At this point, before continuing the discussion of the activities of decision analysis, it would seem appropriate to consider some of the issues which have so far been raised. A number of these will be repeated when the benefits of appraisal are listed, but I would highlight the following at this stage:

Improved communication

By its very nature, through the open discussion of needs and concerns, together with an increased awareness of expectations and aspirations, communication improves dramatically. For all three schools, this was seen as a considerable benefit.

Role agreement

A clearer understanding of colleagues's roles and responsibilities cannot help but enhance closer and more effective working relationships. This was particularly true of School C, where, as will be seen, an option of additional reviewers was developed.

Appreciation

A particular benefit of an appraisal/review process is that it provides an opportunity for showing appreciation for the contributions of the reviewed. Too often, praise and thanks are taken for granted, and it was particularly pleasing to note the pleasure and satisfaction of participants for whom appreciation had been displayed.

Activity	Comment
Reporting Relationships	Cognizance was taken of the complexity of reporting relationships within a school, with additional responsibilities for pastoral and careers activities, for example, forming part of a teacher's working environment. In School A, the pilot group was those with particular responsibility for the sixth fôrm and ranged from a scale one teacher to the deputy headteacher. In School B, the complete (Science) faculty acted as the pilot group and in this instance 'normal' reporting relationships were enforced. The working party in School C comprised a cross-section of school staff which included the headteacher and a part-time teacher. It was in this school that the option of selection of reviewers was introduced.
Communication	A pre-requisite for any hope of success in the introduction of appraisal/review is the communication of activities to all sectors of the organization. To this end, for Schools A and B the following initiatives were taken: 1. Fact sheets prepared and circulated to all staff members whether participating in the exercise or not (fact sheets summarized the proposals and process for each school).

Activity	Comment
	2. 'Surgeries' were held by the writer on two consecutive days in both schools to allow any staff member the opportunity of voicing worries or queries. There were very few visitors and their concerns were with process rather than principle.

This holding of surgeries was viewed as a positive move but a lesson has been learned in their use. For any further exercise of this kind one would not hold them in a headteacher's office. Although the offices had been turned over to my sole use, I believe that they might have been an intimidating factor with a suggestion of hierarchical control. A more familiar location, such as a science laboratory, might have been preferable rather than one associated clearly in the mind of the staff with the senior management of the school.

Activity	Comment
Questionnaires	Developed for all three schools for participating staff. Analysis of the data obtained showed a clear indication of receptivity towards the exercise.
Determination of title	The wording is important. It was found more acceptable to introduce the word 'review' rather than the more emotive 'appraisal' or 'evaluation'.
	In Schools A and B the title was determined as: 'The . . . School Career Development Review'.
	For School C the developed title was: 'The . . . School Professional Development Review'.

Activity	Comment
Process and timetable	The task here was to develop a process which would meet the following criteria:

1.   It should be straightforward in terms of administration while emphasizing the requirements of confidentiality.

2.   The process must be two-way, and allow self-appraisal and the expression of concerns, successes and aspirations.

3.   There must be an opportunity for an exchange of information between reviewer and reviewee which would result in a statement of agreed training and/or development action, plus agreed objectives for the next review period.

4.   There should be some form of appeal procedure in the event of unresolved issues. This procedure could include the availability of some form of 'ombudsman' figure.

5.   For School C there should be a choice of additional reviewers to supplement the comments of the principal reviewer, taking additional responsibilities into account.

6.   The timetable of the review had to be as little disruptive to the school routine and curriculum as possible. Discussions held suggested that the introduction of the process would

Activity	Comment
	prove a disruption whenever it was held. What was agreed was to develop a timetable which was as short as possible, commensurate with the requirements of effectiveness and discipline.
	The timetables evolved, and the actions required followed. It is worth noting that our endeavours matched our planning and the review processes were completed on time. This discipline and commitment was especially commendable when considering the climate of dispute prevalent. The timetables were as follows:

Week one

A. Reviewer hands section one of the review document to the reviewee. This (self-appraisal) section requires the reviewee to:

1. Describe the period under review in terms of achievements and successes, plus difficulties encountered – with perceived reasons for those difficulties.
2. List training and development needs against aspirations.
3. Complete this section within week one.

B. At the same time, during week one the reviewer completes section two which is the reviewer's perception of the period under review, again in terms of achievements and any difficulties.

Weeks two and three

Counselling meetings held between reviewer and reviewee where sections one and two are exchanged, agreed (and amended if required), and section three completed. This section records an agreed statement of the reviewee's training and development needs plus (agreed) objectives for the coming review period.

Francis Arnold

Weeks four and five

Senior reviewer (with the consultant) studies and analyses review documents to determine what responsibility for further action he or she has.

Activity	Comment
Guidelines	The development of guidelines for reviewer and reviewee is essential for any appraisal system. They will obviously vary from process-to-process but have the aim of providing a workable framework for completing the exercise. Examples of these guidelines follow:

A *Reviewee guidelines* (Section 1)

1. Performance	Describe your own performance during the review period in terms of achievements and successes.
2. Difficulties	Include any difficulties you encountered and suggest what help you need, and from whom, to overcome them.
3. Training and Development	Identify any training and development needs you believe you have for your own development and for an enhanced contribution to the needs of the school.
4. Activities	List any extra-curricular activities you have been involved in, also any courses you have completed (with dates).
5. Contribution	Suggest any other ways in which you could contribute your particular skills to the school, and which are currently under-utilized.

6.	*Appreciation*	Where appropriate, please show appreciation for any help and support you have received.

B.   *Reviewer guidelines* (Section 2)

1.	*Performance*	Describe the reviewee's performance during the review period in terms of strengths, successes, problems and needs.
2.	*Objectives*	Comment on the achievement levels of agreed objectives.
3.	*Last review*	Describe what previously agreed action has been completed and what, if any, is outstanding.
4.	*Appreciation*	Include your appreciation, of, and for, the reviewee's contribution both to your department and the school.

C.   It is essential, for the success of the exercise, that both the reviewer and reviewee are as open and objective in their comments as possible (including those on each other).

Activity	Comment
Training	The need for training for appraisal review is apparent – particularly where there is no previous experience of introduction. Training falls into three categories:
	1. Process training to ensure that participants are completely *au fait*

Activity	Comment
	with the mechanics of the process to ensure its smooth completion.
	2. Counselling training (with simulated review counselling interviews).
	3. Listening and questioning techniques to ensure that the discussion between reviewer and reviewee is as productive as possible.
	The use of video recording during training for appraisal proved worthwhile. Feedback and advice have more impact when one has the evidence of sight and sound.
Monitoring and controlling	The process implementation must be monitored to ensure that the discipline of the timetable is adhered to. Any 'slippage' with a loss of impetus will result in a corresponding loss of credibility. As I have stated earlier, it was very much to the credit of the participants in all schools that discipline and commitment to complete the exercise within the timetable was maintained. This particularly applied to Schools A and B when the exercise was held during the difficult period of teachers' dispute.
Issue of post-review questionnaires	Designed to determine the effectiveness and acceptability of the experience with particular reference to the question: 'Having completed the review exercise, would you recommend it to other members of staff?'

Activity	Comment
Training action planning	An analysis of needs and required action identified in order to develop appropriate action planning.
	A number of common needs were identified with a few demands made on the Local Education Authority (who had been kept informed of the progress of the various stages of the development).
Discussions with participants	Held approximately 4 months after the exercise.

Implementation and documents used

Thus the review process in Schools A and B had four distinct phases which are outlined in Figure 5.6. Sections 1 and 2 are carried out by the participant and reviewer independently. Section 3, the counselling meeting, brings together the two parties and leads to the development of a training or action plan which forms the basis for Section 4. An outline of the documents which relate to the first two and the last sections can be found in Figure 5.7. The process in School C was somewhat different and this is described in Figure 5.8.

School C

The basic procedure outline in Figure 3 is repeated but with the addition of the option of the input from other reviewers.

Review of appraisal process

Illustrations of responses to appraisal documents follow but these must be regarded as typical and general rather than specific. They do, however, genuinely represent the positive nature of the responses which had been generated.

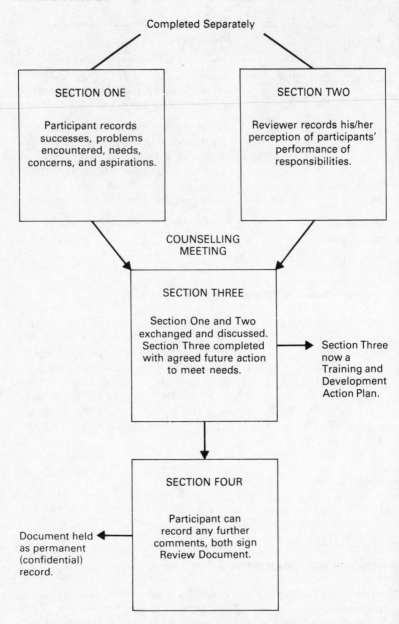

Completed Separately

SECTION ONE

Participant records
successes, problems
encountered, needs,
concerns, and aspirations.

SECTION TWO

Reviewer records his/her
perception of participants'
performance of
responsibilities.

COUNSELLING
MEETING

SECTION THREE

Section One and Two
exchanged and discussed.
Section Three completed
with agreed future action
to meet needs.

Section Three
now a
Training and
Development
Action Plan.

SECTION FOUR

Participant can
record any further
comments, both sign
Review Document.

Document held
as permanent
(confidential)
record.

Figure 5.6   A career development review plan (Schools A & B)

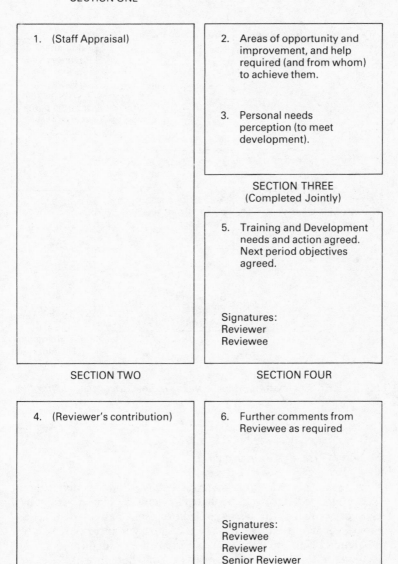

Figure 5.7   Appraisal document (Schools A & B)

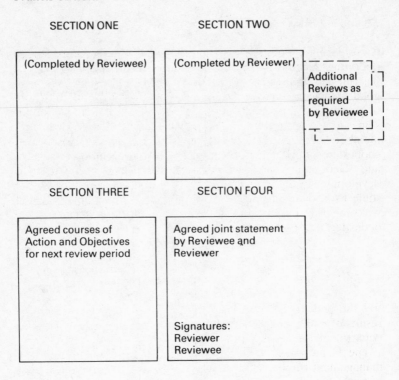

Figure 5.8 Professional development review document (School C)

Section 1 – Head of Department

'During the period under review I believe that the department has progressed during difficult circumstances. Union action has caused disruption to classes and the normal pattern of teacher/pupil interaction and relationships. Shortages in resources have heightened our problems but determined and dedicated action has been displayed by all members of this department.

I would like to be able to manage my time more effectively so that less work has to be taken home and meetings and discussions need not go on so long during after school hours.'

Section 2 – Headteacher

'Considering the difficulties under which the school has been operating during the dispute with Government, I find that . . . has run her department very well. Examination results have been good and there seems to be an awareness throughout the school of the service this department provides. I believe that relationships between this Head of Department and her departmental members are good. I would hope to see closer liaison and cooperation between the English Department and Art, History and Geography, and would welcome any joint initiatives developing. In the interests of . . . 's development, I believe that some form of management training would be helpful. Finally, I welcome this opportunity of expressing my appreciation of a dedicated and professional colleague.'

Section 3 – Joint Agreement of Action

'By the end of the next term the Headteacher will receive the results of a planning meeting to improve liaison between the four departments mentioned in Section 3.

The Headteacher will investigate the options for arranging a management training course (which will include the management of time) for . . . .'

Problems

It would be unrealistic to suggest that the introduction of appraisal into schools which have no tradition of appraisal is without problems. The experience from the three schools discussed in this chapter suggests that the following observations encompass the perceived difficulties and disadvantages.

1. The pressure of what is perceived as ever-increasing work demands makes the timing of the introduction of appraisal particularly acute. The standard response was that there was not, nor ever would be, a convenient time. For Schools A and B the period agreed upon was March/April and for School C, September.

2.   There is concern about the ability of the reviewer to actually meet agreed and identified needs. Should this be the case then the credibility of the process will be in jeopardy, and there is likely to be a loss of commitment to further involvement. Fortunately, this did not prove to be the case with this experience and emerging needs were dealt with within the resources of the schools and the writer.

3.   There may be suspicion, because of past problems or relationships, and a reluctance to accept change.

4.   There may be a reluctance on behalf of the reviewee to admit to difficulties, for fear of the use to which this information might be put. This was appreciated and it would be facile to suggest that practice will soften the concern. I believe that the process of separate completion by reviewer and reviewee does merit support. Unlike certain industrial appraisal models, where the reviewer does not write anything until the reviewee's input has been received, the processes I have outlined do aid the reviewee's honest comment with an emphasis on the identification of the reasons or causes for any difficulties encountered.

5.   Appraisal does require honesty and objectivity in comment. If the process is to provide benefit, that benefit can only be brought about by the expression and acceptance of concerns, followed by agreed action for their resolution. Blandness will achieve little.

6.   Completing an appraisal exercise is inevitably a drain on those prime resources of people and time. There is no way of obviating this problem, of course, but what proved essential was the application of participants to the discipline of the agreed timetable. Discussions were held as to the possibility of providing cover for staff involved in the exercise. If the entire staff is to participate then complete cover is clearly unlikely. The reality is that time has to be found, in spite of other demands, and of the conditions of service proposed. It was also apparent that the shorter, intense timetable was preferable to a protracted exercise which could lead to a loss of impetus and commitment.

Benefits

1.   The process does improve knowledge and understanding of concerns and needs. This understanding will improve relationships and can be a very heartening event.

2. As a communication exercise it is difficult to beat. The feedback received from participants was unanimous in acknowledging the benefit of honest and objective communication.

3. Successfully completed, appraisal is a motivating factor in its own right. My experience is that it can generate a positive corporate spirit of awareness and commitment.

4. Appraisal is a safeguard for the appraised. The vacuum of assumption I previously mentioned is dispelled and there is an available record of opinion and commitment which the individual can refer to. This is a valuable document which is 'on call' for references, applications and discussion.

5. The process provides an ideal, and often long-awaited, opportunity for expressing appreciation. Time often obstructs opportunity for more than fleeting praise; appraisal focuses and records specific appreciation for contribution.

6. Pure objectivity is near impossible to attain, but a process which includes self-appraisal and an exchange generates an objective environment for development.

7. The reviewer's commitment to the growth of the reviewed is an affirmation of responsibility which is under scrutiny and monitoring. The very fact of the reviewer having recorded his or her agreement to take action to meet needs ensures that responsibility cannot be shelved or unduly delayed.

8. The activity of developing a process which is appropriate to the ethos of the school does generate a strong sense of shared ownership.

9. Job responsibilities are confirmed with the opportunity for updating personal information – such as training completed.

10. Appraisal is the natural and desirable extension of the continuous observation and review which the manager completes. The counselling meeting provides a focus for fresh knowledge and commitment.

Conclusion

The results, happily, confirmed the desirability of introducing appraisal. The benefits experienced by the schools involved outweighed the (understandable) concerns and suspicions, and many fears and shibboleths have been dispelled. I would, therefore, recommend the introduction of staff appraisal review to anyone considering it by summarizing the following key elements:

1. It is, in spite of its emotive connotation, a unifying activity where development and ownership is shared.

2. As a communication exercise within departments it is particularly effective. The exchange of views and concerns lead to greater understanding of needs and aspirations.

3. It is management practice which displays that acceptance of responsibility for assisting in the development of staff, and in so doing provides the (often rare) opportunity for demonstrating awareness of effort and difficulties, and expressing appreciation.

4. Properly trained for and executed, the process of appraisal is a motivating agent through improved relationships. The agreement of further objectives and action strengthens links between reviewer and reviewee with its joint acceptance of responsibilities.

5. It is a safeguard for the reviewed where recorded and available comment replaces any feeling of uncertainty or assumption.

6. The role of the 'outsider' to help and advise in the development of the process has been justified.

Finally, I would express my appreciation of the receptivity, skills and generosity of three very committed and impressive head-teachers: Eunice Phillips, Richard Nosowski and Jim Wilson.

Chapter 6

Whole-School Evaluation and Staff Appraisal in Secondary Schools

S.M. Slater

Introduction

I shall attempt in this chapter to draw out for the reader my views of whole-school evaluation based on considerable work carried out during two headships, as chairman of a working party to develop a new authority document on evaluation in the Metropolitan Borough of Solihull, and as a partner in 'Evaluation in Education.' The latter partnership has organized a range of national conferences and published a *National Journal on Evaluation* for a number of years.

I should, at this early stage, record my thanks to all those colleagues who have added to my knowledge and experience in this field. Evaluation is, of course, a corporate professional exercise and cannot be carried out in isolation. It is, then, a way of looking at our school, the management structure, school curriculum and the professional development of the staff. Evaluation should, no, must, become an accepted formal part of school routine, its aim to improve performance in all areas of school life.

We should build on the informal frameworks for evaluation which already exist within all schools. Time does not permit us to develop a new and expensive superstructure nor to dally with ideas that do not pay off. The multiplicity of pressures that we face each day in school will not cease while we erect new and complex systems. We should then use sensitively the management structures and responsibilities which staff already hold within our institutions. This may not be as difficult as one might expect; however, the process does require considerable in-service training as well as negotiations with staff. It also requires us to be clear about the terminology which we choose to use. In this chapter, therefore, I shall use 'evaluation' to refer to a systematic review of a school in terms of its procedures and achievements, based on its aims, objectives and targets. Appraisal is the assessment of performance of staff based on the context within which they work. A 'section' is a part of a school for which a senior or middle manager has responsibility.

It is important to emphasize that staff appraisal can only be viewed as forming part of a whole-school approach to evaluation and professional development. Viewed in isolation staff appraisal can only be damaging, rather than the rewarding process it should be when integrated into a coherent whole-school programme of evaluation. Staff appraisal is about making people feel bigger not smaller.

What follows, then, must necessarily be seen in relation to the structures and patterns which exist in particular institutions. We must bear in mind that we are dealing with individuals in the service who vary in expertise, experience and commitment. We must, therefore, build on our staffs' strengths, be sensitive but resolute in our determination to improve quality and performance in our schools by developing formal systems for evaluating our work. No one system or scheme of evaluation will suit all schools: an important part of the process is to allow schools to discuss, negotiate and develop their own system. Ownership and commitment to the process of evaluation is essential and rewarding. Fruitful ways of approaching the area of evaluation and appraisal have thus been identified.

Reasons for evaluation

There are many reasons for embarking on evaluation and it is essential that staff are aware of these. However, three common aspects can be established. Firstly, it is a means of establishing an understanding of our current position in relation to our aims and objectives. Secondly, it allows us to redefine, where applicable, our aims and objectives, therefore improving our effectiveness and efficiency. Finally, it is a means of accounting to an external agent about our performance. The understandings held by staff of why we should evaluate will clearly be reflected in the variety of perceptions and roles of those within the education service. Therefore, at LEA level the emphasis may well be placed on the need to be able to make efficient planning decisions in relation to the provision and allocation of resources, and to be able to identify staff training needs across the authority. At LEA level the need to be able to account for policy decisions, to report and justify proposals for forward planning will be an essential outcome of evaluation, and so on.

At school level, evaluation will be regarded as a continual process of evaluating how well the aims and objectives of the school are being met. Therefore, it is essential that agreed and fully negotiated aims and objectives are followed by all within the institution. At whole-school level we will wish to review our curriculum provision both formal and informal. This will allow us to be in the position of being able to judge whether our curriculum is broad based, coherent and balanced for each pupil, encourages and teaches pupils to learn, reflects the changing demands of society, and enhances each child's personal and social development. It is also important at this level to be able to judge whether we provide effectively for staff support and encouragement by recognizing, praising, and disseminating good practice, improving professional communication systems, identifying needs for in-service training, and identifying areas of weakness and devising means of support (Solihull 1986).

We would also wish to be able to make judgments about the management and organizational structure of the school. Evaluation at the level of the whole school will finally also enable us to satisfy the proper demands of accountability. At section level the identified reasons for evaluation may well be different but there will be common areas, such as reviewing the aims and objectives of the section, reviewing the management structure and roles/responsibilities of staff, developing strategies for departmental INSET and so on. However, there will be a focusing on individual teachers so that the process of evaluation will enable them –

To extend and develop their own teaching styles and strategies.
To agree common areas and shared priorities within the section.
To develop strategies for effective use of materials in the classroom.
To assess the suitability of material.
To assess the effectiveness of pupil assessment procedures.
To improve classroom management skills.
To be able to account for current practice.

It is therefore essential to remember, when embarking on

evaluation, that different views and expectations will be held by staff at different levels within the service about the reasons for evaluation. The most important point is that it must deliver personally to all those involved in the process by improving the quality of their performance through professional development.

As is fitting, I have dealt with some of the many internal reasons for embarking on whole-school evaluation. However, there is a range of external pressures on schools which reflect directly on the school itself. Indeed, perhaps the term 'external' is inappropriate. Figure 6.1 is an attempt to summarize the pressures which are influencing our schools and moving us closer to the need to undertake formal evaluative procedures. The reader will, I am certain, wish to include others. However, for the sake of space, I have focused on four main influences; educational, economic, societal and political. During the 1980s we have seen mounting pressure from the DES to develop formal evaluation/appraisal schemes at local Authority/school level. The year 1985 was an important one in the development of thinking in terms of evaluation and appraisal. *Better Schools*, (DES, 1985a) stated that regular and formal appraisal of the performance of all teachers is necessary if LEAs are to have the reliable, comprehensive, and up to date information necessary to facilitate effective professional support and development and to deploy teaching staff to the best advantage.

In the same year, the HMI publication *Quality in Schools: Evaluation and Appraisal*, (DES, 1985b) and the Suffolk study *Those Having Torches: Teacher Appraisal – A study* (Suffolk, 1985) also offered further pressure. The 1986 Education Act and the 1987 Teachers' Conditions of Service (DES, 1987) have made evaluation and appraisal an integral part of our professional duty.

We do not have 'options': evaluation and appraisal must now be seen as a 'common core' element to our work and development. School life is indeed dynamic and complex. It has always required careful planning and monitoring. However, this must no longer be seen as an informal process, rather an explicitly stated formal process. As a headteacher of a school moving to full financial autonomy, the necessity for us to enhance and develop our present system of school evaluation is clear if we are to ensure educational quality and financial efficiency. Recent Government proposals may well see further developments in this area of financial budgeting to all secondary schools.

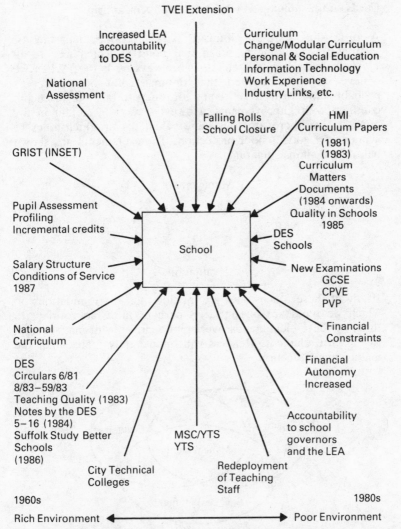

Figure 6.1 shows the following pressures directed toward the central box labelled "School":

TVEI Extension

Increased LEA
accountability
to DES

Curriculum
Change/Modular Curriculum
Personal & Social Education
Information Technology
Work Experience
Industry Links, etc.

National
Assessment

Falling Rolls
School Closure

HMI
Curriculum Papers
(1981)
(1983)
Curriculum
Matters
Documents
(1984 onwards)
Quality in Schools
1985

GRIST (INSET)

Pupil Assessment
Profiling
Incremental credits

DES
Schools

Salary Structure
Conditions of Service
1987

New Examinations
GCSE
CPVE
PVP

National
Curriculum

Financial
Constraints

DES
Circulars 6/81
8/83−59/83
Teaching Quality (1983)
Notes by the DES
5−16 (1984)
Suffolk Study Better
Schools
(1986)

Financial
Autonomy
Increased

MSC/YTS
YTS

Accountability
to school
governors
and the LEA

City Technical
Colleges

Redeployment
of Teaching
Staff

1960s   1980s

Rich Environment ←——————————→ Poor Environment

It should be noted that the mounting pressures on schools has taken place within a backdrop of changing economic circumstance for the education service. The relatively high resourcing of the 1960s and early 1970s has been gradually eroded and replaced by a more stringent climate.

Figure 6.1   Pressures to review the work of schools

Cards on the table: good schools – the piecemeal trap

As professionals we are all aware that our schools, departments, sections, etc. can never reach that point at which we are all satisfied, because good schools can always be better. When we believe we have reached that optimal point of quality it's probably time for us to retire and for others to take our place and continue with improvements. However, what is certain in my mind is that there are four major elements or touchstones to achieving a good school or section. These elements are shown below in a simple diagram.

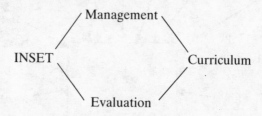

If any of these touchstones are missing then the foundations on which we build are unsafe. It is perhaps more appropriate to think of these elements as overlapping circles with management as the core element. Readers will immediately realize that the management function

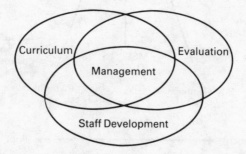

is perhaps the one in which teachers, including headteachers, have received little or no training at all in the past. However, developments are taking place in the profession to enhance our management training, including the setting up of training centres for headteachers, and a range of other courses for all who are prepared to accept the need for training. Some, unfortunately, within our profession seem to reject the need for management training, believing that teaching has nothing to do with management! Perhaps the outcome of this view has been the piecemeal development of our education system over the last twenty-five years. Curriculum development during the 1960s and early 1970s was a cause for particular concern. Curriculum projects were often seen in isolation with no recognition of whole-school developments or indeed of the need to evaluate and monitor these new courses. In many schools the curriculum has developed in an *ad hoc* if not totally unsatisfactory manner. *Aspects of Secondary Education in England* (DES, 1979a) supports this view and this led to much of the pressure to develop common core curricula. Perhaps, more importantly, the piecemeal approach to curriculum development has also been mirrored, in schools, by a piecemeal approach to evaluation.

Evaluation and subsequent change have been crises-orientated, e.g. bad geography results last year mean some changes will have to be made in the geography department. Similarly, the professional development of our teachers has often been pursued in a piecemeal way. 'Teachers go off on courses, disseminate little of what they learn, and the effect of resources expended is seldom evaluated, save by the staffroom stalwart who notices the substitution list.' (Slater and Long, 1986, p.44.) The need to develop a whole-school approach to identifying staff INSET requirements is essential if we are to move forward and develop a coherent approach to professional development. The recent developments in terms of Grant Related In-Service Training (GRIST) will undoubtedly enhance this movement. I would argue that we can overcome these piecemeal developments in our schools by drawing together, through management, whole-school policies on curriculum, staff development and evaluation.

Creating the climate – stage-by-stage process

All major innovations require detailed planning and careful preparation, and those affected need to be involved in this planning and preparation. Evaluation is clearly a major innovation and it is essential, therefore, to involve all staff at all stages in developing the process that will be used in the school. The first stage in the process is the development of commitment by the headteacher. This needs to be followed swiftly by training, which should perhaps be provided by the LEA via residential conferences for headteachers. It is important for headteachers to feel 'comfortable' within the field of evaluation, to understand the reasons for and advantages of formal review, and to be aware of the processes involved in developing a whole-school approach to evaluation.

My own experiences as a head of both academic and pastoral sections of a school, as a timetabler, director of studies and deputy head in charge of school evaluation were excellent training grounds, as was my postgraduate training in management and qualitative/quantitive research techniques. Fortunately, ten years on, we are better placed to develop more formal training sessions on evaluation and appraisal, such as those within my own education authority. The headteacher, then, has a responsibility to train his/her senior staff team (in both my schools this team included deputy headteachers and senior teachers). This can be achieved by formal in-service sessions, discussions and regular meetings of the senior staff team focusing on management and evaluation. It is important that evaluation and appraisal starts at this level within the school, a point to which I shall return later.

The headteacher should then, in partnership with the LEA and senior staff, take on the responsibility of training the senior and middle managers of staff in the principles and techniques of management and evaluation. We have achieved this via weekend residential training sessions. These training sessions are essential in that they set the trend for future developments as well as improving team building skills. The aims and objectives of our weekend conference were clearly stated and working sessions task orientated. (See Appendix 1.) I would argue strongly for residential conferences in that they offer formal and informal opportunities for face-to-face interactions. It is important that all staff are aware that the conference is taking place and that it is part of a process of staff training and development in terms of a whole-school approach to evaluation. It is equally important that staff are aware that they are to be trained/consulted before any such evaluation/appraisal programmes are introduced. This can be achieved in a number of ways through the formal meeting schedule or through specific meetings or papers to staff.

The next stage for creating the climate is to hold similar training sessions for all staff involved in the school. These training sessions must allow for open discussion and interchange of ideas. It is important to allay all fears and to agree on areas such as confidentiality. It is vital to establish an atmosphere of trust and a feeling of security. This can be achieved if all understand that the process of evaluation and appraisal is about professional development and improving the quality of what we offer to our pupils. Headteachers may feel it appropriate, with the permission of governors, to use in-service training days for the purposes of developing plans and strategies for whole-school evaluation. We have used training weekend conferences, occasional days, early closures and meetings after school. Time spent wisely in training preparation, planning and agreement, will pay dividends in the future when the process is under way.

Creating the climate through a staged in-service training programme designed to meet the needs of individuals and sections within the school should enhance the success of the evaluation programme. The important role played by senior staff in leading the initial work on evaluation and appraisal is perhaps one of the key indications to staff that there is nothing to lose or fear from the process. However, it does require confidence and trust amongst the senior staff, hence the need not only for training but also for team building programmes. The professional development programme should also make clear to *all* that staff appraisal or, as I prefer to call it, the professional development interview, is only part of the overall evaluation programme. It is also a *two-way* process between the person conducting the professional development interview and the interviewee. The criteria for appraisal must be negotiated in advance and agreed by the parties prior to the interview. These interviews cannot take place without such planning, material and data gathering, and classroom observation. Indeed, in my experience it is advisable to hold a pre-interview meeting to draw up the agenda for the actual professional development interview, and agree on what material needs to be collected and how this is to be done.

The process

Creating the climate is an integral part of the process of evaluation. It will be through the programme of in-service training that the framework for agreed action will develop. The task orientated residentials, in-service training days, and meetings will cover not only the principal purposes, conditions and outcomes of evaluation, but also the procedures or framework for action to be undertaken. The process developed within my schools has been very similar, relying heavily on the present

STAFFING MATRIX		Head	Dep. 1	Dep. 2	Dep. 3	St. 1	St. 2	St. 3
Staffing	Permanent	X						
	Temporary		X					
	Probationers					X		
	Students					X		
	Welfare) Discipline)	All involved as necessary						
	Develop/Support					X		
	In-Service		X			X		
	Evaluation	X				X		
Timetabling	Main T/T						X	X
	Cover							X
Examination	Organization (external)							X
	Timetabling (external)							X
	Organization (internal)							X
	Timetabling (internal)							X
Curriculum	Curriculum Development		X			X		
	Curriculum Support	X	X	X	X	X	X	X
	Options			X		X	X	X
Pupils	Parents		X	X	X			
	Intake			X				
	Careers					X		
	Discipline	All involved as necessary						
	Standards		X	X				
	Welfare & Support	All involved as necessary						
	Liaison with outside agencies		X	X	X			
	School/Colleges liaison	X				X		
	Withdrawal of pupils from lessons			X	X			
	Pastoral Support	X	X	X	X	X	X	X
Care of Building				X	X			
Capitation/Funds/etc.		X	X					
Furniture & Equipment							X	
Building Alterations		X	X					
Returns		X	X					
Duties		All involved as necessary						
Duty List & Changes			X					
Development of Policies Structures		X	X					
Programme	Centre	X						
	School		X					
PTA			X	X				
Bulletin			X					
Outside Visits			X					
Staff request for absence			X					

Figure 6.2   Staffing matrix for allocating responsibilities in a school

management structures. When senior staff have been trained in the field of evaluation, a framework for action at senior staff level needs to be identified and agreed. This framework will later form the basis for discussion with staff regarding a whole-school approach to evaluation. It will, from our experiences, start with clarifying the school's aims and objectives and then move to the identification of job description and roles and responsibilities for senior staff, including the headteacher. These role descriptions need to be discussed, agreed and published in the staff handbook. It is essential to engage the help of middle managers when discussing the roles and responsibilities of senior staff to avoid misinterpretations and taken-for-granted assumptions.

There are a range of ways to allocate and negotiate roles and responsibilities. However, I have found the matrix approach particularly useful (see Figure 6.2). The headteacher draws up a matrix and asks senior staff either to identify their present areas of work or provide this draft completed as a starting point for discussion. I believe that role enrichment is one of the tasks of headship. It is for this reason that we have role changes after a period of three years. This also allows for future individual negotiations where role changes are agreed by all concerned.

Clearly, if we as a senior staff team, which for me includes the deputy headteachers and senior teachers, are looking at our performance then we must start from the firm base of known role descriptions and responsibilities. The next step is for senior staff to set short-term targets and agree ways of evaluating successes. These short-term achievable targets can initially be team targets (non-threatening) and should be communicated to all staff. Indeed, staff may well be involved in helping to achieve these targets, e.g. pupil promptness to lessons. However, it is the senior staff team's performance that will be evaluated, discussed and agreed by the senior staff team. Once started, the process will undoubtedly gather momentum and early success will lead to target setting as a regular part of management procedures. Individual targets will clearly be based on role and the job descriptions and should be a contribution of short- and long-term prioritized tasks. It is important that the headteacher assess carefully the targets set to ensure that they are achievable. There is initially a tendency to overstretch the realms of possibility in terms of achievable targets. The ways of evaluating performance will be many, quantitive and qualitative (Appendix 2) depending upon tasks set. However, a common element will be the professional development interview (Appendix 3). These two-

Aims and Objectives of the school. (Accepted by all staff.)
↓
Role Negotiation/Clarification and Acceptance.
↓
Corporate Target Setting. (Short Term and Achievable.)
↓
Agreed Evaluative Procedures/Criteria (including Staff Appraisal/Development Interviews.)
↓
Data Collection/Evaluation (i) – new targets set – movement towards individual target setting short/long term.
↓
Evaluation/Appraisal (ii) – professional development where appropriate.
↓
Feedback new targets set. Cycle begins again.

Figure 6.3   A process framework for senior staff

way interviews with the headteacher are based on detailed agendas negotiated and agreed in advance between both parties. Confidentiality will have been agreed in advance of all interviews, including what will appear in writing and what may be placed on record cards or files. However, written outcomes in terms of new target areas for action need to be stated at the interview. Inset programmes and professional development discussions are also set in motion where appropriate. It is always advantageous to have a brief follow-up interview to allow for further comments after reflection. The advantages of these interviews need to be publicized to the staff body as a whole by the senior staff. This can be done by summarizing what has happened at senior staff level: it has been a movement from aims and objectives, to role negotiation; from clarification and acceptance, to target setting, initially team based, then individually; followed by evaluation and appraisal. (See Figure 6.3.)

It will be clear from the process so far that regular formal meetings of senior staff will be an essential feature of the programme. They are, of course, present in most schools. However, these meetings will become perhaps more important as they are now evaluative, discussing the future direction of the school in relation to senior staff targets, including those of the headteacher. Senior staff colleagues will now be aware of their colleagues' targets, thus ensuring no duplication or inefficiencies.

We are now moving towards management by target setting and a team management philosophy. During this process continued professional development and support from the LEA will be an essential requirement. It is also during this stage that it is important to publicize the benefits of evaluation. Indeed, many staff, especially middle managers, will be directly involved in the collection of evaluative data for senior staff. Many staff will also be crucially involved in aiding their senior staff colleagues to set short and long term targets.

The process framework at middle management level

Middle managers will, through the in-service training programmes set in motion by the senior staff team, be aware of the advantages and purposes of evaluation. This, together with the additional feedback from their senior staff colleagues through formal and informal meetings, should make them ready to become involved in a similar process. The starting point is again to discuss and negotiate roles and responsibilities. Here as well the matrix can be useful. Senior staff who have direct responsibility for heads of section will already be aware of how to tackle the procedures of negotiation, having been through the process themselves. Clearly, staff within each section may also be approached by the head of section for feedback about his or her role. Training of senior and middle managers, as mentioned earlier, is important at this stage because they will follow the same procedures as senior staff in terms of setting targets and evaluating their progress. However, since all the staff in the school will now become involved at some level or another in evaluation work, it is essential to embark on whole-school INSET and discussions about the evaluative process to be used in the school.

Whole-school process framework

We have found that, by starting with senior management, staff are willing to see the process as essentially supportive. It also allows the senior staff to develop an expertise in the theory and practice of evaluation before asking others to become involved. It is at this stage, then, that staff development is essential for all staff. If support can be obtained from the LEA/GRIST then a

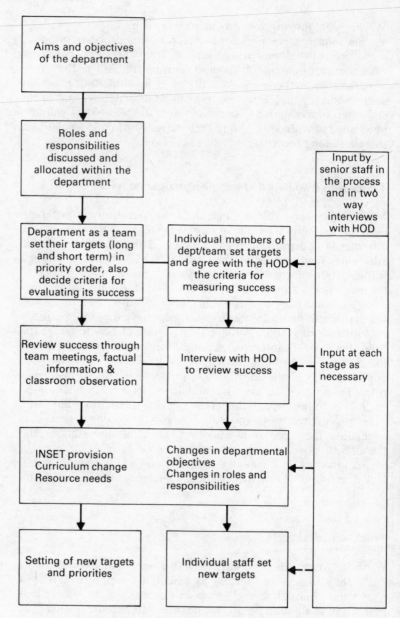

Figure 6.4   The process of review at department level

two-day residential course, targeted to develop a framework for action for staff to discuss, is an advantage. In my first school this residential course identified the framework (see Figure 6.4) which was eventually agreed by all staff after several INSET/ discussion meetings. It focuses on section level but carries the hallmark of the process developed at senior staff level, i.e. setting aims and objectives for the section (which must reflect whole-school aims and objectives), and the use of GRIST for identifying roles and responsibilities, agreeing evaluative procedures and criteria, target setting, review and the stating of new targets. It can also be seen that appraisal interviews are a delegated management function – the headteacher appraising his senior staff, senior staff their section heads, and section heads their staff. It was also agreed that staff could speak to and be appraised by senior colleagues if appropriate or desired.

In my present school, where the process is not yet fully operational due to external pressures, we developed a similar framework at a task orientated in-service training day. The training day was preceded by an in-service training weekend for senior staff and senior middle managers (heads of year/faculty). The framework (Figure 6.5) is indeed similar to that in Figure 6.4, using the existing management structure as the key to the process framework. In both schools the framework was accepted by the staff with the proviso that we might well change elements of the programme if we felt it appropriate.

Recognizing our responsibilities

As suggested elsewhere in this chapter each school will need to devise a programme of evaluation suited to its own particular needs. It is vital, therefore, that this period of staff discussion is well planned and written up. It must allow time to explore individual thoughts, feelings, worries, and to establish the principle that the process is concerned with professional develop-ment of all staff from the headteacher to probationer. It is also important to provide a framework for individual discussions, if required, with the headteacher or designated head of the evaluation programme. It is also vital to ensure that all relevant documentation outlining the process is available for all staff.

By delegating evaluation and staff appraisal to section level we developed a process of whole-school review which was based on present structures within school. No expensive, time consuming

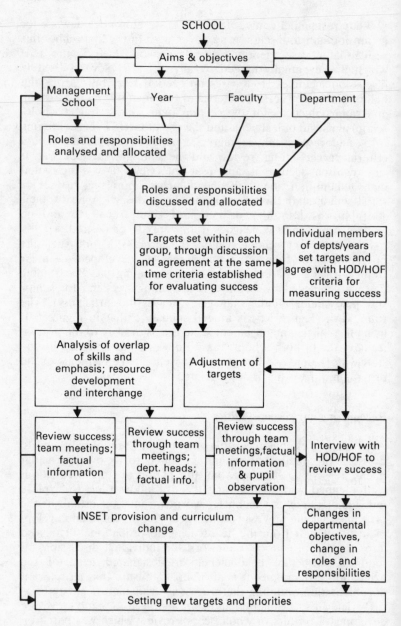

SCHOOL

Aims & objectives

| Management School | Year | Faculty | Department |

Roles and responsibilities
analysed and allocated

Roles and responsibilities
discussed and allocated

Targets set within each
group, through discussion
and agreement at the same
time criteria established
for evaluating success

Individual members
of depts/years
set targets and
agree with HOD/HOF
criteria for
measuring success

Analysis of overlap
of skills and
emphasis; resource
development
and interchange

Adjustment of
targets

Review success;
team meetings;
factual
information

Review success
through team
meetings;
dept. heads;
factual info.

Review success
through team
meetings,factual
information
& pupil
observation

Interview with
HOD/HOF to
review success

INSET provision and curriculum
change

Changes in
departmental
objectives,
change in
roles and
responsibilities

Setting new targets and priorities

Figure 6.5   The process of school review

100

superstructures needed to be erected, and teachers felt at ease working within a framework with which they were familiar. It also meant, perhaps for the first time, that senior and middle managers and their teams recognized their full range of responsibilities. Heads of section were required to negotiate aims and objectives, clarify roles and responsibilities, and review their work, which included observing their staff teaching (senior staff providing cover where necessary). However, before the latter could take place, department and pastoral teams had to discuss the criteria for good lessons and performance (surely an essential requirement of all teaching teams?). Classroom observation like the appraisal interview was, of course, two-way, heads of section being observed by their staff. It should be re-emphasized that staff appraisal cannot be viewed in some kind of theoretical isolation since we all work within those teams as part of section review. However, staff appraisal must be well planned (see Appendix 3) and staff must be fully trained in how to carry out the interview.

Recording and reporting

Once the framework for action is agreed by staff, be prepared for a vast increase in the demand for professional development programmes at individual, section and whole-school level. Areas for training, such as target setting, classroom observation, report writing, curriculum review, two-way staff appraisal, management and many other needs, will soon be identified by staff engaging in the process framework. This provision is vital if we are to respond quickly to these professional demands of our staff.

Having developed a framework for agreed action it was important to work towards the production of our annual reports for section managers, headteachers, governors and LEA. The report was used to identify a range of important matters, including review of last year's work and, vitally, future plans for action in some considerable detail. The headings of the reports were as follows:

1. School philosophy/aims, objectives.
2. School resources – staffing, buildings, capitation, etc.
3. Section reports Department/Year areas
   (a) Aims and objectives
   (b) Staffing – roles/responsibilities
   (c) Curriculum schemes of work

      (i) Successful areas

      (ii) Areas in need of improvement

      (iii) Changes anticipated.

(d) Assessment procedures/pupil profiles/external examinations

      (i) Suitability

      (ii) Areas for improvement

      (iii) Changes anticipated.

(e) Resource allocation

      (i) Suitability

      (ii) Changes desired for future

      (iii) Bids for extra resourcing with evidence.

(f) Rooming/Timetable

      (i) Suitability – advantages/disadvantages

      (ii) Desired changes for next year.

(g) INSET/Provision

      (i) Courses attended team/individual

      (ii) INSET needs for next academic year.

(h) Priorities for action

      (i) Last year's priorities reviewed

      (ii) New priorities set.

The head of section, together with his or her staff, will then produce the report over a period of time, usually in the summer term, for presentation to myself and the deputy headteacher in charge of school evaluation. However, it is important to stress that this document for the year is based on an ongoing programme of target setting, curriculum review and staff appraisal. In both schools, I and the deputy head or senior member of staff responsible for the pastoral and the academic sections of the school carry out in-depth interviews with the heads of section based on their reports. It is then our job to compile a full school report for our own purposes and for the purpose of accountability.

Conclusion

My experience suggests that by engaging in evaluation, we improve our motivation, and performance at all levels. It is a prerequisite to good management, coherent curriculum development, and staff training. As a profession we have nothing to fear from evaluation or appraisal. It provides for us, in terms of accountability, with a recognition of our efforts. However, more importantly, it enhances the educational provision that we offer to our pupils. It is for this reason that we must all include evaluation and, therefore, appraisal within the 1,265 contractual hours.

Chapter 7

Whole-School Staff Appraisal in the Primary School

A.J. Richardson

Introduction

Systematic curriculum and school self-evaluation within primary schools is still generally uncommon – despite the impetus of local authority based initiatives and national developments such as Guidelines for Review and Internal Development in Schools (GRIDS) and the work of the Suffolk team in *Those having Torches* (1985). Less common still are evaluation structures or systems within primary schools which address how primary teachers carry out their complex roles as class teacher, post-holder/curriculum consultant, specialist, manager and so on. In 1983 HMI noted that some self-evaluation was taking place in 56 LEAs although at that time only 11 had mandatory procedures requiring the production of written reports (DES, 1985b). Since this time there has been a marked increase in these kinds of activities, whether they be school or LEA based. *Better Schools* (DES, 1985a) also had much to say about how the Government intended to introduce legislation requiring LEAs formally and systematically to appraise the performance of teachers. The recent Education Act (1986 No. 2) confirmed this and it is only a matter of time before some sort of national teacher appraisal system is developed. Certainly, since April 1987 teachers and headteachers are bound by imposed conditions of service which make such an appraisal system possible and likely.

It is within this context that the evaluation/appraisal scheme at Green Lanes has developed. A key feature of the processes which have evolved in the school over the last three years is that they are part and parcel of a continuous programme of whole-school development. HMI commented in 1985 that,

. . . teacher appraisal appears to work best where the school as a whole is accustomed to looking critically at its practices; and certainly the evaluation of curricular, pastoral and other provision is given more substance and credibility if it includes an assessment of the functions and performance of individual teachers.
(DES, 1985b, p.47.)

This assumes, of course, that the school has successfully arrived at the point where the staff can openly address curriculum and pedagogic issues together, and have developed a collegial approach to the development of the school. This is difficult to achieve but it is an essential prerequisite to the development or adoption by the school of systems for professional teacher appraisal. It is difficult to achieve because in many primary schools the autonomy of individual teachers is a dominant ideology.

Even in so-called progressive open primary schools, teacher autonomy appears to dominate. Sharp and Green's study in the mid-1970s illustrated that the common vocabulary of progressive education employed by primary teachers, that is the use of phrases such as 'stages of learning', 'child-centred', 'pupil autonomy and decision-making', seemed to operate as badges or ritual symbols of commitment to the political structure of the school. The rhetoric of openness, self-evaluation and child-centredness appeared to function in staff discussion but not in the classroom, where teachers protected their individual autonomy by proclaiming their tacit agreement with the school's dominant ideology at staffroom level – leaving them free to operate as they liked in the classroom. (Sharp and Green, 1975.)

It is not suprising that this should be so. Primary schools have tended to be organized around the single class-teacher model. This teacher is generally responsible for the planning, preparation, delivery and evaluation for what counts as the curriculum for the individual pupils in his or her care. In some schools there are team teaching or exchange arrangements but, in the main, the quality of the education that the pupils receive is a direct consequence of the quality of the work of the class teacher. Thus, in most primary schools, the structural organization of the school tends to programme the extent to which individual teachers are willing to participate in self- or collective evaluation of classroom work.

This chapter will describe an approach to staff appraisal which has developed during the last three years, within the context of 'whole-school' evaluation and curriculum development. During this time an attempt has been made to develop within the school a context and platform for review and evaluation of our professional work. I take the view that teaching should provide a research opportunity for all teachers. Every time we teach or work alongside children or colleagues, we are making a series of mostly intuitive judgments about what is going on. The best kind of teaching is that which capitalizes upon these judgments in order to enhance children's learning opportunities and to address what the Schools Council termed 'curriculum match'. This judgment should inform the planning, delivery and organization of the curriculum and of the structures operating within the school. This may seem an obvious point to make but, in my experience, it is uncommon for these intuitive judgments to acquire any real substance. They tend to be lost within the immediacy of the classroom and are rarely utilized in professional planning. This chapter will illustrate an approach to enabling these 'judgments' to become more systematic and consequently, more useful.

Establishing a professional context

The process of teacher appraisal should be the natural and logical consequence of developing the school and the curriculum. The key aims of the process should be the enhancement of educational opportunities for the pupils and professional opportunities for the staff. To try and achieve this it is essential that a context to facilitate the professional development of colleagues is created. Despite the apparent openness of many primary schools, the act of teaching remains an almost private act for many teachers. Discussion of how we teach is taboo. How can the curriculum be developed without influencing or changing the way teachers teach? The simple answer is that it cannot. When I was appointed to Green Lanes in 1984, discussion of how we teach, what we teach or why we teach was not occurring. This was mainly due to the lack of a context within which to discuss this. The school had eight classes and a 60-place nursery. Each unit within the school operated largely in isolation. The curriculum was, on the whole, devolved to individual teachers. A major feature identified by staff was the lack of continuity between classes but somehow this issue had not been collectively addressed. I took the decision that before any changes were proposed in the professional work of the school, I needed to define my role as headteacher in terms of facilitating and initiating an evaluation process. I said that I would (and I spelt this out in writing) spend approximately three days each week working alongside teachers and children throughout the school in order to begin the process of making an assessment of the learning needs of the children and hence the curriculum needs of the school. It was also made clear that the end result of these teaching, observation and subsequent discussion sessions would be to identify the points at which pupils' needs were being successfully met. I also emphasized that the starting point for this assessment needed to be how the pupils were operating within the curriculum. Although my presence was initially perceived as a threat to some staff, I found that I was quickly accepted because I deliberately tried to play a helpful 'classroom assistant' role. I worked with children and assisted the staff.

Clearly, I was soon in a position to begin to assess pupil learning needs, social needs, the possible resourcing needs and the quality of teaching and organization in meeting these needs. Having pre-stated that it was my aim to enable all staff to participate in the process of beginning to identify curriculum priorities for subsequent development, this early class-based involvement enabled specific discussion to occur between myself and individual teachers, grounded upon the immediacy of the classroom experiences. However, it will also be clear that generalization from specific classroom discussion following a particular lesson or session can be problematic. I therefore decided to publish an explicit agenda for discussion, focusing upon four key issues. These were:

1. *Continuity* – in terms of curriculum continuity, continuity of pupil experience, and continuity of school and classroom organization and routines.

2. Our *Expectations* of pupils and the relationship between this and our perception of their needs. Indeed, what processes operated in our teaching to enable us to build a picture of individual or collective pupil needs?

3. How were we making *Assessments* of pupils at both a formal and informal level?

4. Identifying exactly what we were *aiming* to achieve through our organization of the classroom and school and our teaching.

It also seemed to me that it was vital that a structure and setting for professional communication within the school was established and seen to operate effectively. Under previous administrations, staff professional discussion had been rather *ad hoc*. More formal discussions, say at staff meetings, had generally taken place at lunchtimes, without an explicit organization, and tended to focus upon issues peripheral to teaching and learning in classrooms, such as sports day or the Christmas concert. These meetings were not minuted. Following individual discussion, I asked the deputy head to take responsibility for convening and recording monthly whole-staff meetings. It was decided that these meetings would profit from being properly run with a prepublished agenda, open to staff input, and that discussion should be recorded in the form of notes and minutes. I also asked that staff should meet together in newly created curriculum planning teams to prepare and review work. From the outset, these meetings were organized on a quid pro quo basis and were given high status by being structured into the end of the school day. (I take half the school for a 25 minute assembly/story session whilst the junior staff start a planning meeting. Infant and nursery staff also meet on a similar basis.)

Distinct advantages have accrued by establishing curriculum and staff meetings on this basis. Everybody knows why the meeting is taking place, approximately how long it will last and, crucially, all staff have had an opportunity to raise matters of concern by putting them on the agendas. Moreover, starting the curriculum meetings in school time means that a good 50 minutes to an hour of discussion can take place by about four p.m. Over a period of time the regularity of meeting has meant that important issues have been properly addressed and vital decisions have been taken – accelerating the professional work of the school. It is also important that at least part of every meeting takes place without me, as headteacher, being present. My absence states clearly my trust and confidence in colleagues as professionals as well as providing opportunities for discussions on matters that perhaps would otherwise not get aired if I were present. In management terms, the regularity of these weekly meetings means that important issues are addressed and returned to if no action has followed. They provide a productive pressure upon me to support developments suggested by colleagues. The most important function of these meetings, though, is their role in facilitating the process of critical and constructive professional discussion. It enables shared meanings to develop and to be understood, and facilitates the testing and examination of ideas which can lead to changes in practice.

During the first term I was in post, I also established a senior management team of the four scale III teachers and the deputy head, whose function was to lead the professional work of the staff in terms of curriculum review and development. This, in fact, had a negative effect and served to polarize views within the school and actually hindered development. I think this was essentially due to lack of role definition and cohesion within the team, which in turn was a function of my misinterpretation of staff needs at this time. What the staff needed and wanted was a common purpose and a feeling of working together, not working in units, as this had been their past experience for the previous several years. So faced with this I gently let the meetings drop after the first couple of terms.

Now, clearly, much of this happened because I 'pushed' it. It seemed to me that it was vital that for the school to develop, time and opportunity needed to be provided for teachers to develop, certainly within a structure which required that particular issues be addressed. The structure needed to provide a learning opportunity for the staff. This learning opportunity centred upon the notion of 'reflexivity', that is looking critically and professionally at our practice. This kind of development can require a tremendous shift for many teachers who have traditionally protected their autonomy by the avoidance of professional discussion, especially in relation to how they actually teach.

Aims, objectives and review

By December of the autumn term of 1984, I produced a detailed discussion paper concerned with aims and objectives which drew upon my own observations and the assessments and emerging issues that were beginning to be identified by staff. This discussion was also informed by the availability within the school of evaluation 'guidelines' such as GRIDS (Bolam et al., 1984) and Solihull LEAs 'Green' booklet (Solihull, 1980). Having said this, only passing reference was made to these documents and they certainly did not provide an immediately accessible means of

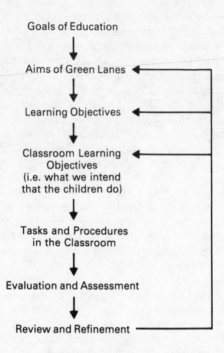

Figure 7.1   Model for school development

promoting and extending staff discussion. However, one or two
staff looked carefully at these materials and raised issues such as
the organization of posts of responsibility within the school. The
aims document emphasized the following model for future
development and provided a consistent and systematic structure
for organizing our professional discussions.

Clearly, within this process, lesson analysis based upon
observation of what is actually happening is essential. Indeed,
observation and lesson analysis is central to the evaluation and
appraisal process – it is the fulcrum of the whole process. At the
same time as this kind of more systematic planning was beginning
to be addressed I began individual discussions with staff in order
to try to identify what they saw as priorities for development.
These meetings also facilitated discussion about scale-post
responsibilities. This led to some agreed redefinition. The end

Aims for the Headteacher

1. To supervise and manage the teaching and deploy resources in such a way that children are taught efficiently and effectively.

2. In cooperation with the school staff and the LEA Inspectors, and Governing Body, to make explicit the school's aims and to see that the curriculum, teaching methods, classroom and school organizations serve them.

3. To ensure that staff are provided with essential equipment and resources in order to carry out their teaching, scale post and extra curricular duties efficiently and effectively.

4. To enable the school to be kept in touch with educational developments in the fields of nursery and primary education.

5. To assist the professional development of teachers and provide opportunities for school-based, LEA and national in-service training.

6. To promote curriculum developments within the school and to suggest and promote teaching strategies which fulfil the school's stated aims.

7. To promote continual curriculum evaluation and review in the light of changing educational needs.

8. To ensure effective liaison with secondary schools.

9. To provide accountability to the Governing Body and the LEA for the aims, organization, teaching methods, and evaluation of the school.

10. To foster good relations with parents and the community and to interpret the aims of the school to them.

11. To ensure the general welfare of all connected directly with the school.

12. To keep records of the development of the school as an educational institution.

13. To evaluate the work and progress of the school.

Figure 7.2   Aims for the headteacher

Language Development Scale III Postholder

Aims
1. To assist the headteacher and the staff to make explicit and interpret the stated aims of the school through the language curriculum.

2. To enable the staff to fulfil the aims and objectives of the language curriculum.

3. To advise the headteacher of the resource needs of the school in the field of language development.

4. To review the effectiveness of programmes of work in relation to the needs of the pupils and the school's stated aims and to advise the headteacher accordingly.

Objectives
1. To enable the staff to be kept abreast of developments in the field of language teaching by:
    (i)   Personal example.
    (ii) Informal and formal staff discussion.
    (iii) The publication of internal discussion documents.
    (iv) Working with members of staff in classrooms, assisting teaching and establishing models of good practice.

2. To develop detailed classroom learning objectives and programmes of work for all aspects of language work within the school, towards the development of an explicit language policy.

3. To develop the notion of 'language across the curriculum' as an integral part of the school's work.

4. To advise the headteacher as to the resource requirements of all aspects of language work throughout the school.

5. To encourage a continual re-examination and review of programmes of work, teaching methods and curriculum aims, in the light of changing educational needs.

6. To organize screening, testing and diagnostic procedures in language throughout the school, in close consultation with the headteacher and the post-holder for special needs.

7. To ensure effective liaison with secondary schools.

8. To be responsible for the care, maintenance, and storage of all language materials and to establish a central language resource area.

9. To be responsible for the care, maintenance and storage of all 'library' materials and to classify these materials using a Dewey based system.

10. To develop child and parental assistance in running the school's library and bookshop and in the care and repair of the stock.

11. To assist the headteacher in interpreting the aims of the language curriculum to parents by:
    (i) The running of curriculum workshops.
    (ii) The involvement of parents in the school's language programme.
    (iii) The publication of booklets for parents which assist and advise parents about children's development in language.

12. To encourage and develop self-supportive learning by enabling pupils to have access to the school's language resources and by making the aims of the language curriculum explicit and intelligible to pupils.

Figure 7.3   Aims and objectives of a language development post-holder

results of these sessions was a clearer view of staff perceptions of priorities for development and the production of negotiated and detailed job descriptions. Figures 7.2 and 7.3 are examples of this 'end' result – my own and a scale III post-holder's job description.

A logical consequence of the creation of job definition was the self-setting by staff of termly targets for professional work. I asked that these targets should match with our agreed priorities as well as being realistic and achievable. These targets, like the job descriptions, were and are published and circulated to all staff, so that the whole process of what we are saying we are intending to do is made explicit to everybody.

Curricular developments

An interesting and parallel development within the school at the same time was the focusing upon pupil involvement in self-assessment and the planning of work. During the spring term

1985, the school was successful in obtaining funding from SCDC to promote this work. Since this time the school has begun to develop a detailed record-keeping and profiling system which actively structures pupil involvement into the process of evaluation and planning.

In its simplest form, our nursery pupils are being encouraged by teaching staff, NNEBs and parental helpers to use language to plan out a small section of their work or play or an activity in which they are about to take part – for example, using sand and water in a particular way. After carrying out the activity, children are encouraged to talk about – to review in a simple way – what they have been doing.

In main school classes, pupils have regular opportunities to review their work and progress through a record system which structures their involvement. The records have been constructed so that key aspects of the work programme are made explicit to children in a way appropriate to their level of understanding. Mathematics and topic work records for example, consist of a series of 'I can do' or 'I understand' statements which in mathematics are linked to resource references. All pupils throughout the school also compile a work profile – a personal file – which comprises a selection of the child's own work which is selected jointly by the teacher and pupil.

The important point about the records and the personal files is that they provide systematic opportunities for teachers and children to review learning. This clearly facilitates the processes of future planning by teachers as well as raising the status of the learner – the child.

Within the context of the development of evaluation and appraisal within the school, this curriculum innovation has tended to reinforce the positive climate for the processes of self-evaluation and self-criticism which were increasingly being directed towards improving the learning experiences of children through translating our explicit curriculum aims into reality.

Teacher appraisal

The initial period of whole-school review, the setting of agreed aims, the redefinition of posts of responsibility, the production of job descriptions and the early initiation of self-evaluation systems for pupils, took about fourteen months to establish. By November 1985, I had already had a couple of target review meetings with individual members of staff. These meetings were quite successful and useful in that they enabled specific discussion to occur, related to scale-post responsibilities and, inevitably, some attention was paid to learning issues. The trouble was that the aspects of the discussions that related to teaching and learning were rather vague – issues of teaching methodology were not addressed head-on but skated around. It seemed to me, and to two other members of staff, that we should attempt to make these review sessions more specifically focused upon teaching and learning – as in the event, scale-post responsibilities could be discussed with ease and focus. The discussions needed to be more concerned with the actual practice of teaching. To attempt to meet this need I decided to discuss the teacher appraisal issue with all staff individually and subsequently produced a short document which attempted to identify a possible 'agenda for discussion'. This document (Figure 7.4) was then quite openly considered at the weekly curriculum team meetings.

Staff welcomed this initiative, I think, partly because it did seem to be the logical extension of what we were already doing and partly because many staff colleagues could see that the appraisal 'writing was on the wall'. At this point I decided to invite my school inspector/adviser to appraise me as I felt that the future success of our developing evaluation scheme would partially depend upon me being subject to the same appraisal pressures as the teaching staff. An agenda for discussion, based largely around the initial discussion document, was agreed at a full staff meeting and appraisal discussions were fixed to take place in school time. It was also agreed that outcomes of the discussion would not be recorded and that the key purpose of the discussion was to facilitate a self-evaluation process for both the member of staff and me as head. In my view it is vital that agreement should exist about the range of the appraisal discussion well in advance. Moreover, it is clear that without a mutually agreed willingness to focus on the issues arising from the agenda, attempts to arrive at a shared meaning of the evaluation and appraisal process would be difficult to achieve.

Although there was some staff anxiety in taking part in this formal discussion, all staff agreed that once the appraisal discussion itself actually started, they felt they were able to relax and begin to address themselves to important issues in a confidential context. Essentially, the discussion provided an opportunity for colleagues to express what they thought about their jobs, the children they were teaching, and organizational

---

Appraisal and Evaluation

Much has been said about the appraisal of teachers in recent months. In this school we are already establishing a system for evaluating the work we do. So far we have:

Developed detailed curriculum aims and objectives for the school which have been agreed by all staff.

Established job descriptions for posts of responsibility.

Set ourselves termly 'targets' for professional work (post-holders).

It seems to me that we could now begin to think about ways of extending and clarifying this process. The following areas could be considered by staff for review, evaluation or appraisal:

1.   The extent to which we have met our post-holder targets.

2.   The effectiveness of our planning and preparation.

3.   The effectiveness of our teaching in relation to the needs of the children and the aims of the school.

4.   The extent to which the aims of the school are being met.

5.   The need to revise and/or develop our aims.

We need to consider the following issues

a)   The aims of the process and result of such an appraisal or review.

b)   Who should 'do' the reviewing?

c)   The form the appraisal should take, e.g. written, verbal?

I would welcome your comments before the December staff meeting.

AJR November 1985

Figure 7.4   Appraisal and evaluation

aspects of the school. Many staff commented that they enjoyed hearing my views about their work within this formal context and that they appreciated the opportunity to sit down with me and have an undisturbed conversation about their views of their work and the school. The fact of the matter is that although we might think we are providing staff with opportunities to discuss their work at other times, the reality of school means that very often these unplanned conversations never really develop sufficiently to permit the kind of detailed professional discussions that had begun to happen in the appraisal sessions.

From my perspective in conducting the interview, I wanted the process to be comfortable and as non-threatening as possible for colleagues. I was therefore as positive in my comments as I could be and tried my hardest to listen rather than talk. Getting these initial interviewing strategies right is absolutely essential if you as a manager are really going to be able to encourage staff to relax enough to be genuinely honest with themselves.

In February 1986, following a staff review of the processes and practices we had thus far adopted, the 'agenda for discussion' was extended and six key areas were identified as relevant for professional discussion. These were:

Planning and preparation
Teaching
Special responsibilities
INSET needs
Career development
Suggestions for improving the school

Each of these categories was explicitly broken-down into several sub-sections. For example, under planning and preparation the following areas were seen to be relevant:

(a) Forecasts of classwork to be covered each half term.
(b) Contributions to infant and junior meetings.
(c) Contributions to staff meetings.
(d) Contributions to informal discussion about classwork.
(e) The teachers' assessment of the usefulness of individual and team planning.
(f) Use of resources.
(g) Record keeping and pupil profiling.

Under 'Teaching' such issues were considered as, curriculum match, classroom organization, relationships with children, class control and discipline and the appropriateness of teaching and

APPRAISAL/EVALUATION RECORD POST: Curriculum responsibility for Language Dev + library

NAME: A.N.Other   DATE: March '87

POINTS/AREAS DISCUSSED

TR commented that A.O. had achieved a very high standard of professional work with class 8. Despite the learning difficulties within a large section of the class, A.O. had provided pupils with a well matched stimulating programme of work. A.O./T.R. discussed A.O.'s recent exchange to Browns Lane JaI - although had proved interesting professional opportunity had not lead to a permanent move to entirely different setting.
Future possibilities:
- transfer to another school,
- application for other, positions on the same grade
- application for position as support teacher under GRIST.
Continuing work on written language policy for school discussed.

AREAS FOR FUTURE WORK OR DEVELOPMENT

① A.O. needs to develop management expertise with other staff - will apply for a management course (like the DES regional course currently being run at Sans Souci) T.R./A.O. to discuss this aspect of A.O.'s work more fully.
② Meeting arranged with inspector for staff development to discuss future career aspirations - T.R. to confirm date.
③ T.R. will support A.O.'s application for similar positions or for support teacher post.
④ A.O. to produce 1st draft of policy discussion documents by April 10th.

OTHER COMMENTS OR POINTS

T.R. thanked A.O. for her work and again commented upon the high standards of her work and performance during the last term-and-a-half.

A. N. Other
(TEACHER)

A.J. Richards
(HEAD TEACHER)

Figure 7.5   Recording the appraisal

learning 'style'. And out of the discussion about these categories, the need for some sort of record of the appraisal discussion emerged. Through individual discussions with all staff, the kinds of areas and comments that might usefully be recorded were considered and a draft document was presented to a full staff meeting for discussion. The final document (Figure 7.5) is very open but reflects where we as a staff are currently in the developmental process of constructing a professionally useful appraisal/evaluation scheme. Access to the document is strictly controlled and the whole process is confidential to the member of staff and me. (The 'sample' given in Figure 7.5 has been written especially for this chapter.)

I think it is likely that our record will evolve to become more detailed but I strongly feel that the rating scales common to some American teacher appraisal schemes are totally inappropriate for the kind of dynamic, human relationship context within which teaching, learning and staff development operates in schools.

Principles, strategies and questions

Whatever teacher evaluation and appraisal does, it should not dehumanize management. I believe that properly developed, over time, in cooperation with teachers, and certainly not imposed, it will act as a vehicle to enhance professionalism, raise the status of teachers and headteachers and improve learning for pupils. Essentially, teacher appraisal should be about providing systematic opportunities for teachers to learn from their practice in order to improve learning for pupils. It should also be about raising morale, the recognition of hard work and success, and the creation of self-supporting development structures within school for teachers.

Headteachers and senior teachers involved in the establishment of evaluation and appraisal in schools need to develop their interpersonal skills in order to facilitate the learning processes that arise through such professional discussion. We need to find ways of structuring time into our work to enable professional issues to be handled. Certainly, in the primary school sector we have not been good at this. Planning and preparation time is given generally low status and opportunities to develop evaluation processes and systems are uncommon. We need to raise the status of planning and preparation by altering both the structure of school organization and by developing away from the dominant ideology of teacher autonomy. Collegiality needs to be created so that staff within a school can have real opportunities to think about and influence learning.

Developing the processes of teacher appraisal and evaluation within Green Lanes has raised a number of important problems. These problems are concerned with management, organization, and the means by which pedagogy and learning is assessed. How can the primary school be organized and staffed to enable teachers to have opportunities to take part in whole-school evaluation? Who should initiate the processes? Who should the results of evaluation and appraisal be known to? How can pupils contribute to the evaluation of learning within the school as it effects them? What should the role of the governing body of parents be? Indeed, what roles are possible or desirable? If a national system of teacher appraisal is introduced; are schools and LEAs equipped to derive benefits – or will the results of top-down appraisal, as an apparent accountability exercise, be wholly irrelevant? Such issues may well be resolved during the next two years when the DES responds to the findings of the pilot schemes currently being established and sponsored. What is clear, however, is that schools which have taken the opportunity to consider the implications and consequences of evaluation and appraisal, as a natural development of their professional work, will be in a sound position to respond positively and forcefully to challenges that may come from Governments in the future. Two key questions should be considered:

- Has the process enabled a teacher to feel valued, professional and successful?
- Has learning improved for the pupils as a result?

Chapter 8

The Introduction of Staff Appraisal to a Newly Amalgamated School

Jenny Morris

Introduction

The amalgamation of three schools would not normally be considered a propitious occasion for the introduction of staff appraisal: nevertheless, amalgamation, like drowning, concentrates the mind exceedingly and in this case focused it positively on the morale and well-being of staff. School closure and the redesignation of staff had been trauma enough; but the rapid development of a new learning environment and the welding together of three sets of staff from schools of differing philosophies, posed particular problems which had to be solved as soon as possible for the sake of the pupils if no-one else.

It was crucial that members of staff fully understood the philosophy and objectives of the new school; they had to understand, and, hopefully, be reconciled to their new designations; and above all they had to feel that they were important, integral parts of a totally new, but immediately viable community. Anxiety and stress manifested themselves in antagonism, indifference and cynicism on the part of people who had been under 'threat' of change for several years, and who now felt their worst fears would be realized. Few members of staff had worked in a school of 1,500 pupils, two of the existing schools were single-sex establishments, the third school had not had selected pupils or a sixth form. The new building was large and as imposing as the situation itself, and few members of staff felt content at the prospect of such apparently gigantic changes.

My area of responsibility had been described as staff development and clearly this held part of the key to successful amalgamation, but only if the development was coherent, valued

121

and appropriate to both staff and school. It was typical of the amalgamation syndrome that the majority of members of staff felt grossly undervalued. They had had no wish for amalgamation and felt their opinions had been overruled. The schools to which they had given so much, were to be closed, thus their efforts and expertise had been judged to be wanting. In vain, did officers and senior staff point out the realities upon which the amalgamation decision was based. Staff perceptions were centred on personal and collective failure, lack of appreciation, and uncertainty of worth.

Uncertainty was fundamental to the entire operation, including my own approach and area of responsibility. I had read the James Report which virtually invented the term 'professional tutor', yet in spite of its recommendation that no school should be without one, within the immediate time span, I failed to find one. I later realized that this shy, retiring species was, in fact, almost extinct before it had properly come into existence. The timing, the habitat and the necessity all demanded the generation of a whole new genus of adviser/managers, but the vital financial spark had not been struck. Even today, I believe I am the only officially designated professional tutor in the area (if not in the county at that time?). I had read a number of books which included staff development as a chapter within the main topic, but practical advice was virtually impossible to come by. Staff appraisal was a phrase used to describe some nebulous process whereby a teacher's 'development' or 'progress' might be 'measured'. Clearly the two had to be linked, but the method had yet to be discovered and time was short. The final package was the result of a very wet half term and fourteen years' experience as a deputy head. I would not claim to have invented the wheel – as I discovered during the following year that others had had thoughts along similar lines before and after me – but this wheel was mine. It was greatly reassuring to have the encouragement of the staff development advisory team from a nearby county to whom I was later introduced, but at the beginning I felt very isolated within my new role.

As professional tutor I saw my first responsibilities, in essence, as being:

1. To reassure staff of their value to the new school, and, where possible, soothe individual anxieties.
2. To ensure that staff understood the philosophy of the new school.

3. To ensure that staff appreciated and understood their individual roles.
4. To discover the professional needs of individuals.
5. To discover the training needs of the new departments.
6. To involve individuals as much as possible with the planning and organization of the new establishment.
7. To discover individual strengths and weaknesses.
8. To encourage commitment at all levels.

The only way in which these aims might be achieved would be by personal, individual contact, given time, quiet and unthreatening surroundings. Simplistically, if you want answers, you have to ask questions and listen carefully to what you are told. It was also clear that these eight objectives were so significant that the questions should be asked on a regular basis – thus was created staff professional review.

Staff professional review

Eight months before the new school opened its doors, a programme of individual discussion was begun. Every member of staff with a role to play at Ashlawn School was invited for a personal discussion with the designated professional tutor. Approximately 80 teachers were involved; invitations were informal and personal, but time had to be negotiated within the three existing schools so that staff could feel relaxed and unhurried. Any further pressures had to be avoided at all costs. A hasty, interrupted discussion would have been worse than none at all. Over-sensitive members of staff needed a calm atmosphere and time in which to express their real anxieties and expectations. It says much for the professional commitment and concern of the senior staff in the three existing schools that such time was given. The head and staff of the school at which I was deputy head, were unfailingly supportive and, I believe, felt that by indirectly 'hosting' the staff of the other schools, they were contributing considerably to the well-being of the new, as was indeed the case.

The word 'interview' had been carefully avoided as being loaded, and even sinister, at that time. Discussions, therefore, were voluntary, though in practice, all but two members of staff accepted their individual invitations. There was no documentation at this time, but the discussions were carefully structured beforehand, to include: the eight objectives previously indicated, an introduction to the idea of an annual staff review, and an opportunity for individuals to introduce topics of their own choosing. Most conversations lasted about 40 minutes, though a number extended well beyond that. It was, I believe, advantageous that I .had been a deputy head in the area for some considerable time and therefore enjoyed a certain status in the eyes even of those with whom I had not yet worked. My job specification was staff development with no obvious curriculum or pastoral responsibilities; demonstrably I had no axe to grind; my questions were seen therefore as being non-threatening and carrying no loaded implications, an important factor if honesty is to play a real part in staff appraisal. Careful staging of interviews, a sincere concern for the well-being of individuals, and a realization that I was seeking to negotiate rather than impose, all served to make the discussions fruitful and generally satisfying.

Initial reactions to the idea of such discussions varied from cynical disbelief in their value (or even existence!) to openly expressed pleasure that 'someone' was going to listen, at last . . . Significantly, it became clear that for the majority of teachers this was the first opportunity they had been given to discuss their job at length with someone who had the status to negotiate desirable changes, but who was in no way judgmental. For most people there had been very few occasions when their professional opinions had been consulted as individuals, and even fewer occasions when they had been asked how they felt about their working situation. Staff had given me details of their qualifications and teaching service, and it had a salutary and saddening effect to see well-qualified, long-serving, dedicated members of the profession expressing pleasure and gratitude for a 40 minute discussion relating to those interests closest to their professional concern. The term 'pastoral care for staff' was coined by one such member of staff who had spent many years caring for the welfare of his pupils, and this, I believe, is as good an expression of the true motivation toward appraisal as we are likely to discover. If that is, indeed, the genuine foundation upon which an appraisal system is based, then members of staff need have no anxieties about it.

A great deal of very useful information was forthcoming from this first round of discussions. Unexpected talents and interests were revealed and qualifications and expertise hitherto unknown became apparent. For example, one music teacher had, outside school, a great involvement with multi-cultural education; a languages teacher had acquired not only an interest, but real

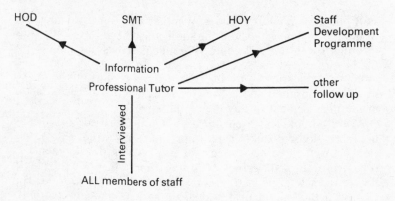

Figure 8.1   Review: round one

expertise in devising exam timetables; a head of year produced some excellent ideas on the development of the library into a whole-school resource centre; a member of the special needs department had an interest and skill in teaching communication – this was to be encouraged, and resulted in a communications module to be used throughout the school. Unknown to anyone, a number of members of staff had completed courses on pastoral care, counselling and active learning – all skills to be utilized and passed on. Frequently, it appeared that individuals had attended courses, and acquired skills that had not been fully utilized at the time, and later had been overlooked. Anxieties were expressed and a surprising number of misapprehensions needed correction. In spite of great numbers of newsletters, etc. staff remained uncertain of the objectives of the new school – clearly the weight of paper compared very lightly to the personally spoken word. In times of stress (and others!) people simply do not read what they are given (especially in schools?) or they interpret as they choose. A great effort had been made to inform staff of decisions and plans, yet a number remained resolutely ignorant until they were obliged to discuss specific issues on a personal level.

When introduced, the idea of an annual professional review greeted with unanimous approval, though a very small (four) indicated anxieties on behalf of 'other' people. expressed agreement with the notion that individual were likely to prove useful not only to members of staff but the school as a whole. Whether such universal approval would have been achieved if the subject had been raised at a staff meeting, for instance, I doubt very much. A mass meeting is not the best of occasions to introduce a matter of such personal and individual concern. As it was, each member of staff felt he or she had been consulted and his/her opinions noted – a crucial factor in the management of any global initiative.

At the end of each discussion a brief note was made concerning interests, skills, possible career ambitions or current dissatisfactions as well as wishes for further professional development. In some cases targets were set for the time which would elapse before the school opened, others were much longer in term. But clearly, if the role of professional tutor was to retain credibility and the implementation of professional review was to be seen as a practical force in the management of the school, there had to be much more than a series of pleasant chats. At first, there was little that could be done, apart from informing designated heads of department of staff anxieties or confusions, and encouraging positive communication between staff. There had been the normal, anticipated reticence between heads of department within the three schools, and those designated who were still obliged to have a foot in two camps. Consequently, the easing of communications made a great deal of difference in the evolution of new curricular and pastoral areas.

A number of teachers were far from happy with their prospective roles and the chance to express these grievances was felt by several to be a great relief, especially when the new roles were considered in a positive light and attention drawn to their proper value; if this could be reinforced by the initiation of a responsibility-related task, aggrieved teachers were able to begin the journey toward self-realization and the achievement of work satisfaction. Often, members of staff simply needed the stimulus of challenge that the objective observer could perceive in the new role, and which the designated teacher had been too anxious to appreciate at the time.

Even at this early stage, the groundwork was laid for future initiatives. Teachers were introduced to others of differing status and curriculum areas, who shared the same interests; and groups were formed, which were to develop of their own volition into working parties, creating programmes for communications and media studies, the modular curriculum, pastoral development and others. These loosely formulated groups did much to fost the ideal of 'one' staff, as well as encouraging the conviction t' staff were not only to be consulted, but that they should begin to take the responsibility of innovation.

There were a number of responsibilities which had not, at that time, been allocated for one reason or another. Surprisingly, for virtually every one of these tasks there was a member of staff keen to take up the responsibility. Without individual discussions many teachers, undoubtedly, would have failed to express their interest, or if expressed, it might not have been noticed by the appropriate people. Staff who wanted experience in pastoral work, administration or curriculum development were thus given opportunities they previously had only hoped for, and it was a source of considerable satisfaction to all concerned when staff and responsibilities could be thus easily reconciled. Indeed, there was a phase when some members of staff imbued the professional tutor with qualities more appropriate to the role of fairy godmother than professional counsellor; however, as is always the case, there are some wishes that no-one can cause to come true, and one or two instances of apparent 'failure' kept the professional tutor's feet firmly on the floor. Staff development may be quite potent magic on occasions, but miracles are still uncommon. Though a certain level of satisfaction was achieved by virtually all members of staff, there was undoubtedly a small number whose sole consolation was self-expression, but this in itself appeared to fulfil a long-felt need.

At the end of the discussions the professional tutor and, therefore, the senior management team, was in possession of a wealth of information. This information was:

(a) To act as a guide for a staff development programme for the first year.
(b) To inform accurately about the need to renegotiate certain areas of responsibility.
(c) Focus management attention on the organization of the pastoral structure.
(d) To assist and guide management decisions during that first difficult year after amalgamation; and
(e) To give an invaluable guide to probable staff reactions to different initiatives.

Another by-product was an appraisal of the skills required by the professional tutor. Patience, good organization and the ability both to communicate and listen were only part of the job. It was necessary to have a clear picture of the structure of the school and a deep understanding of its principles and management. It was necessary to be able to negotiate at all levels and remain encouraging and positive, regardless of expressed anxieties or antagonisms. It was also important to know what was possible and what should not be considered as likely or desirable. Discretion was the paramount virtue, combined with the ability to assess that which was genuinely confidential and that which was intended to be passed on.

Two months after the opening of the school, the county authorities requested a bid for funding the school-based, in-service training. This was not only heaven-sent as a staff development opportunity, it was to provide the proof that staff professional review worked. A programme based on already perceived needs was funded and put into practice. Not only was it greatly appreciated by the participants, but it gave many members of staff the opportunity to pass on their acquired expertise in a number of areas. Without review, neither the needs nor the providers of training would have been recognized.

In-Service Training included:

(a) Training for staff interested in teaching pupils with special needs.
(b) Pastoral care and counselling.
(c) Information technology.
(d) Visits to other schools.
(e) Review workshops.
(f) Reference-writing workshop.
(g) Management workships, etc., etc.

The second professional review

The second round of professional review required a more formal structure if ideas, requirements and expertise were not to be lost. A file was established for each member of staff; it contained a summary of the individual's service record and staff development, notes on the original conversation were included. This file was totally confidential, being in the safekeeping of the professional tutor who would allow no access without the expressed permission of the member of staff it concerned. Surprisingly, the majority of staff felt this to be of little significance. Clearly, professional review held few fears for them, though a very small minority reacted very strongly to the idea of confidentiality and needed considerable reassurance. Also significant was the fact that an increasing number of staff referred to the process as appraisal, though great care had been used throughout to stress the review aspect of the procedures. Once again, participation was voluntary and the majority of staff took part, though Union pressure meant that some, though willing, felt unable to participate.

The core of the programme consisted of 4 documents: 1 to be completed by the individual member of staff; 2A to be completed in conjunction with the head of department/faculty; 2B to be completed in conjunction with the head of the year; 3 to be completed in conjunction with the professional tutor.

In each case, if an individual preferred he or she could choose another member of staff, e.g. second in department for these discussions – though this option was not, in fact, taken up.

Heads of department were reviewed by the curriculum overseer, that is, the member of the senior management team, responsible for an oversight of that subject area. Deputies were reviewed by another member of the senior management team and the head; the head being reviewed by a senior county adviser. In the future, the head might be reviewed by another head, and adviser, and a more junior member of staff in order that there might be feedback from those being managed.

A variety of formats had been evaluated, including a number of 'tick-in-the-right-column' questionnaires. These were all discarded as being too confining and the eventual formula was as follows:

Document 1

Question 1 referred to both teaching and pastoral roles and asked the reviewee to discuss those aspects which were felt to have been most successful. Question 2 referred to areas of dissatisfaction. Question 3 related to professional development. Question 4 asked if further help or advice would have been useful. Question 5 discussed objectives to be set by the individual for him/herself. Question 6 asked if help would be required to fulfil these objectives, and if so, in what way could the school and/or staff assist; and the last question discussed personal aspirations.

Documents 2A and B

Followed a similar parallel pattern.

Document 3

Largely a summary of objectives and INSET requirements.

It should be noted that documents 2A and B referred directly to a job specification – rather upsetting if the reviewee did not have one! As the creation of job specifications had been one of the subjects embraced by the first round of talks, few difficulties were, in fact, encountered. Needless to say, these days the precise nature of each job specification must be carefully negotiated for purposes other than appraisal, but an examination of the exact nature of individual roles is useful for both the staff and those who seek to 'manage' them.

Obviously, one of the biggest problems was simply time. Each of the discussions took approximately 30 minutes and each head of year or faculty had approximately 11 members of staff for whom he or she was responsible. The professional tutor was responsible for organizing the timing in a general sense, and kept control of documents for the sake of confidentiality and in order to ensure no-one was missed, but the deputy responsible for the operation of staff cover had to be clear what his priorities were, and one decision had to be that the head's review was seen by the head as being of sufficient importance, that during the summer term it took precedence over other demands on staff non-teaching time. The fifth year leaving made life easier in that respect and the time thus available was virtually given over to staff review. Needless to say, without the head's positive support, the operation of any scheme of appraisal is virtually impossible. Not only does it become inoperable in the practical sense, but if there is resistance from the head on philosophical or other grounds, then perceived changes or initiatives will not occur and any possible satisfactions will be lost; the programme loses credibility and becomes yet one more target for the staffroom cynics. The review process took approximately 6 hours of staff time in total per person; the professional tutor using roughly 3 hours per member of staff in organization, discussion and follow-up.

Once again, this round of discussions yielded valuable information, some of which was very gratifying indeed. The great majority of staff had, for the most part, settled comfortably in

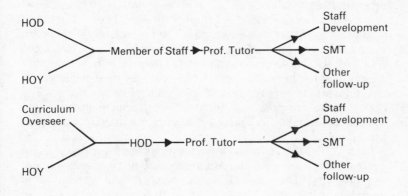

Figure 8.2   Review: round two

their new roles, and were more than satisfied by the challenge and stimuli these roles, and the new environment offered. The staff development programme was not only appreciated but was beginning to pay dividends in greater confidence, improved skills and a unity of commitment and purpose which had previously been lacking. There was also a marked improvement in individual self-image.

Members of staff had not simply been told that they were valued, but had been encouraged to take initiatives, devise development programmes and create their own opportunities for improvement. This paid handsome dividends in improved self-confidence and motivation. However, the second round of the review had taken on a new dimension; one which had not existed in the preliminary stage. The school was actually in existence, so members of staff knew the realities of their situation, but further than that, were now discussing these realities with their immediate managing colleagues. The professional tutor was no longer a filter (or barrier) between heads of department and other members of staff, or between heads of year and their pastoral teams. The discussions were direct, though hopefully not confrontational and not all heads of year and faculty had prepared themselves properly for this new situation, though most handled it admirably with practice.

Appraisal is very much a two-way process, the individual having the right to express opinions about the management of the establishment without fear of 'reprisals', and all staff exercised that right in a constructive and thoughtful way. Thus a number of organizational changes were made and procedures modified; which not only satisfied the critics but which were clearly the result of staff-motivated initiatives. Perhaps this is yet another reason why the head and deputies of a school must have a clear commitment to appraisal and a willingness to listen. The opportunities are presented for good management practice, but sometimes it takes courage to change traditionally accepted procedures.

Once again, the staff development programme produced itself, while the door was opened for a number of interesting changes of responsibility. The school, like any other, had a number of vacancies to fill during the year, as well as operating a policy of job-rotation, so that, in a falling-roll situation, it was very useful to be aware, in advance, of individual interest in different responsibilities. Opportunity arose for a head of year to assume the responsibility for the library and resource centre; the deputy who was head of upper school assumed responsibility for curriculum planning; the second in the special needs department assumed responsibility for the oversight of students within the school; the assistant to the first deputy took responsibility for the development of pupil profiling. Where promotion points are concerned, the job is clearly a subject for interview, but a member of staff indicating interest and preparedness to train for a post *before* it exists is clearly concerned and well-motivated and deserves careful consideration.

However, one difficulty manifested itself quite quickly during this second round of professional review: the skills necessary for an in-depth, constructive discussion were not necessarily those previously required by good heads of year, and heads of faculty. When returned, the written documents varied considerably. One head of year produced perceptive, sensitive reports with imaginative and stimulating recommendations for further development, having had structured yet relaxed discussions which had clearly generated a great deal of interest and enthusiasm within each member of his pastoral team. At the other end of the scale, as one member of staff, rightly aggrieved, expressed herself, 'my entire year's work was dismissed in one line . . . ' and 'we had a nice chat, but . . . '. Clearly, such a disparity of skill and practice would do little to enhance the reputation of review as a motivating, organizational force. Accordingly, a review workshop was arranged for all heads of year and heads of faculty. This was intended:

(a) To strengthen the perceptions of review as a management tool.

(b) To re-inforce the understanding of the middle manager's role.

(c) To remind pastoral and curricular heads of their responsibilities with regard to the professional development of staff within their care.

(d) To develop awareness of the need for interview skills.

(e) To help develop those skills.

This proved to be a very valuable experience for all concerned. It was the first occasion when all head of year and faculty came together with a common purpose, concerned solely with a concept relating only to the new school. In itself, it was a useful, interesting afternoon, generally much appreciated and enjoyed. For some, the idea of management training within the school, and by the school, partly in school time, was a novelty, yet it set a tone for future training which was invaluable. Not only were managers being treated according to their status, they were learning, together, to handle a new, clearly valuable instrument for better organization. As one head of faculty wrote in a later report on the workshop. 'I very much appreciated being *treated* as though I were truly a manager. It's no good telling me I'm important, if I'm treated like an office-boy. Yes, I did enjoy the atmosphere and the refreshments – not just because I liked the cakes, but because they showed that I and my colleagues were worth taking the trouble over.' Hopefully, some skills were learned as well! Certainly, the quality of both discussions and reports improved considerably.

Another workshop was held for staff in charge of smaller departments, and assistant heads of year, with similar results, and a further, slightly different workshop is planned for other members of staff who have indicated a wish, simply to know more about appraisal, or who hope, in the future, to have a direct involvement in the process itself. Obviously, the greater the number of opportunities for training, the more involved and confident staff become, but, as with the introduction of appraisal, such training is clearly more successful in fairly small groups.

Classroom performance evaluation

From this second round of discussions emerged, perhaps not surprisingly, a request for classroom performance evaluation. Though this was clearly desirable, I had hesitated to introduce such a principle without careful planning, and this is where a structured appraisal programme had again proved its worth. During the life of the school it had become common practice for classroom 'visitors' to be encouraged. Curriculum overseers regularly visited the classes of those members of staff within their designated areas; team teaching was a frequent practice; pupil-tracking and curriculum surveys all served to promote an 'open door' policy, which meant that the idea of classroom performance evaluation was both a logical progression and a reasonable appendage to a general review process. There was no stigma attached to having a visitor, and no sinister undertones. Indeed, visitors were made welcome and often invited to comment on what they had seen and heard. Individual discussions about classroom evaluation had produced very encouraging responses, many members of staff seizing quite eagerly upon the idea and urging that it be adopted. Yet if such a procedure had been suggested in an open staff meeting, I doubt whether its passage would have been anything like so easy – there seems to be an 'aura' of imposition about such situations, which cannot be present in individual discussions, added to which, of course, there is the opportunity to listen to the feelings and opinions of *all* staff, as opposed to hearing the responses of only the most vociferous.

A series of questionnaires was devised, relating to classroom evaluation, and offered to a number of 'volunteers' who completed the forms on their own behalf, as a self-evaluation document. Once again, the 'tick-in-the-box' format was discarded by unanimous decision, in favour of a series of questions relating to performance, preparation, relationships, etc., which required a written answer. This questionnaire will be offered to staff during the next round of review as an 'optional extra', and has been so constructed that it may be self-evaluative, or the member of staff can invite whomever he or she wishes to perform the evaluation after visiting one or a number of lessons.

Embarking on the third round of appraisal, is, therefore, comparatively painless: a letter is sent to all staff, reminding them of procedures, and those unfamiliar with the documents, etc. have a chance to discuss the scheme individually before it begins. Sadly, teacher unions are not entirely supportive of our efforts and some colleagues will participate in only a limited fashion, nevertheless, the principle will have been upheld, that *every* member of staff has the opportunity to discuss their personal professional development with a senior member of staff, even if complete participation is deemed impossible for some.

Conclusions

Even in spite of, or because of, amalgamation and current low morale in the profession, appraisal is demonstrably one of the most valuable management tools as yet devised for the creation of a commited, contented staff – *if* it is used properly, with the right attitudes and by the right people. But it must not be forgotten that appraisal can be a powerful instrument with a very sharp edge, and the same implement can create either a masterpiece or a heap of dead wood, depending on who wields it. Lack of genuine sympathy and professionalism will render appraisal every bit as fearsome as many teachers imagine it to be, as will lack of commitment on the part of the head. Appraisal takes time, resources and care; if the head is not willing to support the system in every way, then such time and effort as is given will be wasted. All the time and trouble that may be lavished on appraisal will also be dissipated if the head and senior members of staff are unwilling to listen to and learn from the results of appraisal discussions. This is a two-way involvement and those who are afraid to face criticism of their own management skills may find appraisal a difficult procedure to follow. Needless to say, in the near future, when staff appraisal becomes an acknowledged and structured part of a teacher's professional life, then some commitment must be expected from LEAs. Whatever system is used, if it is to have any meaning, then it will demand time, training and resources and should not simply be added to the already monumental list of deputy head's duties. Clearly management structures need careful examination in every school where it is intended appraisal should occur. The member of staff responsible for appraisal, should, I believe, have deputy head status, but should not, in addition, be expected to be head of upper school or in charge of curriculum planning, as well as staff-cover, duties, school-fund, etc., etc., etc.

Jenny Morris

Handy hints for deputies OR What I have learnt in the last two years

1. Make sure *you* know what appraisal or review really is. You may be questioned closely on this topic.
2. Evaluate the commitment of your head to appraisal. The head should be questioned closely on this topic.
3. Have clear in your mind the purposes of appraisal for your school. Are you going through the motions? Is there a genuine desire for a structured plan for staff and school development?
4. Examine your own motives. Do you sincerely believe in a policy of 'pastoral care for staff' or do you really believe teachers should be able to look after themselves?
5. Do you have a clear understanding of the school's aims? You may, directly or implicitly, be questioned closely on this topic.
6. Can you cope with criticism, direct or implied, whether deserved or otherwise? Think carefully about your answer.
7. What processes for both introduction and organization of appraisal are right for your establishment? No two schools are alike and, though you may be tempted, simply 'borrowing' another scheme may be catastrophic.
8. Consider strategies for the introduction of appraisal *very* carefully, before you begin (see chapter 5!).
9. Are you prepared to learn and/or teach new skills?
10. Consider carefully the practicalities of the administration and organization of your scheme. You will be questioned closely on this topic.

Finally, if all goes well, prepare yourself to receive the gratitude of members of staff who have, perhaps, waited years to express their anxieties and hopes, to someone who actually listens and who has their professional well-being at heart.

Chapter 9

Appraisal and the Headteacher

Harry Moore

Introduction

During the 1980s there has been increasing discussion at many levels; national, local and school based, relating to the appraisal of both teachers and, more critically, headteachers. As we saw in chapter 1, assumptions about the objectives of any system of appraisal have been diverse, ranging from a highly threatening 'weed out the weak' and 'more pay for the popular' to attempts at trying to make maximum use of the most important resource we have in trying to improve the quality of children's education. The author's experience in establishing an essentially formative system of appraisal is intended to highlight important practical aspects of the implementation of a scheme – in particular, the vexed issue of the appraisal of the headteacher. 'It sure as hell would lose credibility if the principals weren't evaluated!' (A quote from an American teacher.)

Formal and informal appraisal

Appraisal has always been present in an informal way. In their various different ways, the head, staff, children, members of the LEA, parents and the rest of the community make value judgements about a school and, by implication, about the teaching staff and head of the school. The 1980 Education Act, which gives parents the right of choice of the school to which they would send their child has, inevitably, resulted in some parents making those value judgements which are part of an informal appraisal. Questions such as: 'would you send your child to that

137

school?' represent a highly simplified form of reaction appraisal by the consumer. These apparently superficial forms of assessment should not be dismissed. The minute by minute gathering of impression, views and assessment form part of the contextual background against which a formal appraisal can be made. Indeed, should we assume that formal systems of appraisal are necessarily more valuable than informal ones? Alexander, for example, questions two implicit assumptions: first, that a formal procedure for evaluation necessarily constitutes the most valid form and, second, that the arrival of a formal system of evaluation necessarily heralds the end of an era of non-evaluation (Alexander, 1984). Surely the two are complementary. It is for the headteacher, in consultation with other staff, to decide those aspects of the process which need formalizing and those areas which will be informal.

This chapter, however, seeks to concentrate on issues relating to a formal system of appraisal as envisaged in the 1986 Act, on the assumption that it will be implemented. Following the interesting initial study by the Suffolk Education Authority (Suffolk 1985), the Government initiated a £4 million programme spread over three years in six local authorities. The early results of this survey appear to indicate diverse approaches to the issues of appraisal and it would be presumptious to assume the details of any future measures, particularly with regard to the level of prescription. Suffice it to note at this point that cooperation with some form of staff appraisal is now part of both a head and a teacher's contract.

Appraisal in the context of whole-school development

A system of staff appraisal is not a discrete element in the development of a school. It must be seen in the context of the organization and the individuals who form it. The complex interpersonal relationships which exist within any organization are critical to the appraisal process, as is an evaluation of the school's aims and objectives and an assessment of the balance between individual and institutional needs. Frequent references are made to the centrality of the headteacher to a school's development and his/her style of leadership is therefore an important factor. A predominantly autocratic head might find a prescriptive form of appraisal most appropriate. The direction of the school is retained within parameters which are defined by the head, who controls the agenda for the appraisal process as he or she does for all other aspects of the school's development. A staff who are totally dependent upon the head for direction are, however, less likely to be in a position to make value judgements about their own professional development since it is not within their experience. Alternatively, a staff who are expected to exercise professional judgement and assume responsibilities appropriate to their experience and expertise are more likely to be able to contribute to a form of appraisal based on self-assessment. Blackburn envisaged a similar situation in his assessment of secondary school appraisal. The appraisal interview is a dialogue between two people in which the interviewer enables the teacher to become the active agent in his/her own appraisal (Blackburn, 1986). In this situation the appraisee is being asked to question fundamental issues relating to the nature of the job and the appraiser performs the function of a facilitator who assists in identifying areas of strength which are deserving of recognition, and those aspects of a person's performance which could be improved. Both elements become strong motivators; the one in the form of praise, the other in understanding ways to develop and the means by which that development can be achieved. The sharing of difficulties experienced, and, realistic aspirations for the future, are important for both the individual and his or her place in the institution.

Who acts as the appraiser?

Central to the appraisal process, is the key question: who acts as appraiser? Research evidence (Turner and Clift, 1985) suggests that, at present, the majority of teachers would prefer that their own interview is conducted by the head. There are, however, certain practical implications for the head to consider, particularly with regard to assessing a realistic commitment as to the number of staff which it is possible to appraise. Primary schools currently range in size from fewer than 50 pupils to larger than 500. Consequently, whilst the majority of heads could consider a system which allowed for the annual appraisal of all staff, it may be necessary for heads of the largest primary schools to consider whether it is realistic to conduct all interviews personally. In Thomas' view, reported in chapter 2, 20 is a reasonable maximum number to contemplate; the author's experience would substantiate this view. The extent and depth of any scheme will also impose restrictions. A simple, annual, half-hour discussion about career development may well not impose an onerous burden upon the head but such discussions may take much longer as Bungard showed in chapter 3.

Classroom observation

Can a system of appraisal which fails to address the teacher's classroom performance be really credible? I suspect that this issue of classroom-based observation will be the most contentious aspect when implementing a comprehensive system of appraisal. A return to the concept of self-appraisal, already referred to, may be helpful here. The head, in the role of facilitator, works alongside a colleague and is able, both by a structured observation and through the continuous informal assessment which is constantly being made by a head who is involved in the work of the children, to share in that colleague's development. Aspects relating to the organization and management of the class, discipline, curriculum development and the children's overall development can be dealt with openly and honestly, and achievable goals established for the following twelve months. Once again, an element of balance between formal and informal methods of appraisal will exist. The informal, day-by-day impressions gained as a result of the head's presence around the school, working alongside colleagues, gives a basis to which the more formal observation may be related. Any formal observation loses the aura of a performance since it becomes part of a process of continuous assessment; another piece of the jigsaw. A non-judgemental approach to the process will also tend to encourage an open discussion of problems. It is suggested that the head working in the role of a classroom helper is more likely to be able to contribute effectively. Delaney explored a similar approach in his assessment of teacher appraisal at St Edmund's School (Delaney, 1986). The development of a system of self-appraisal, whereby the head and a member of staff share the process, may evolve into a consideration of alternative approaches involving other staff. For example, the appraisal of a member of staff might identify a problem within the area of language. The head will not, necessarily, be the most appropriate person within the school to support the member of staff. Detailed knowledge of the school's language policy and its implementation may well be most effectively dealt with by the language curriculum coordinator.

The appraisee, appreciating the need for development which is the initial function of the head as appraiser, seeks the guidance of the post-holder who will, in turn, be able to judge the implications for whole-school evaluation in that particular area. Shortcomings in the provision of resources are also highlighted through the process.

Career development

Thus far, the concentration has been on the issues which relate a system of appraisal to the function of the school. Another important aspect of staff appraisal is the development of the individual's career. Turner and Clift found that an important element in many schemes concerned the career development of the individual (Turner and Clift, 1985). The realistic career aspirations of a colleague are the legitimate concern of the head if he is performing the function of leadership. It is important that, for those who see their future within the school, appropriate opportunities and challenges are available, and, for those who seek promotion or further experience elsewhere, guidance is given as to how to achieve such an aim. Although selection and promotion are not an integral part of staff appraisal, it is inevitable that aspects of the process relating to career development will become part of a system for selection.

Negative elements

Much of the foregoing has been based on the assumption that the overwhelming majority of teachers wish to improve their own performance. Many of the issues raised depend for success, on relationships of honesty and trust and the willing cooperation of all involved. It would be foolish to ignore the possibility that undertaking the implementation of so complex a procedure as staff appraisal may result in individual conflict. This could result, principally, for one of two reasons. First, is the rejection, by an otherwise competent member of staff, of the appraisal process because it represents a threat to that individual. One would hope that, with sensitive handling of the situation over a period of time, it is possible to solve the difficulty. Second, and more serious, is when an appraisal involves dealing with an incompetent member of staff. One of the most negative and destructive

141

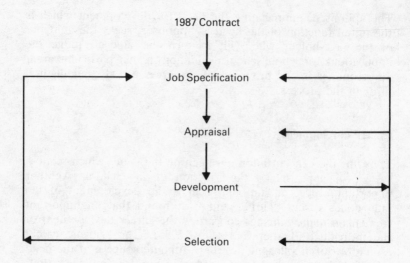

Figure 9.1   The role of appraisal

elements to emerge from the initial debate on appraisal is the suggestion made, most notably by Sir Keith Joseph, that it is to 'weed out the bad teacher'. It is the author's view that such a criterion would negate all the positive aspects associated with the process. If an incompetent member of staff is identified then it is a matter for disciplinary proceedings; appraisal is emphatically not the appropriate procedure to use!

Procedures – establishing objectives and job specifications

The implementation of the *Education (No. 2) Act, 1986*, Section 49 (Appraisal and performance of teachers) which came into force on the 7 January 1987 will necessitate the introduction of a set of procedures. The documentation appropriate to the system of appraisal will require careful thought, and the head, in consultation with colleagues, will have a central role in formulating and evaluating an efficient and effective set of forms. Figure 9.1 sets out a structure to clarify the place of appraisal in the overall process, and shows the cyclical nature of this process. The 1987 *Contract of Employment* (DES, 1987) with all its implica-

---

Job Specification
Class Teacher

To:

1. Provide an environment for all children which is rich and varied.
2. Organise and deploy resources to suit the needs of all children.
3. Establish discipline based in mutual respect and the development of self-discipline.
4. Be aware of the school's agreed curricular aims and objectives and develop each child accordingly.
5. Consult, as appropriate, with colleagues, support agencies and parents.
6. Maintain suitable records and provide reports appropriate to the school's overall policy.
7. Always respond to the responsibilities embodied in 'loco parentis'.

Figure 9.2   A generic job specification

tions for the future of the teaching profession, must provide the starting point because it embodies binding contractual obligations. Figure 9.2 sets out a typical, generic job specification for a class teacher. It naturally follows from the contract since it must satisfy the requirements of that same contract. The centrality of the job specification to the process of appraisal is explored in greater depth later in this chapter, when dealing with the appraisal of the head.

Prior to the implementation of any system of staff appraisal, it will be helpful to discuss, plan and prepare a set of guidelines which are broadly acceptable to all colleagues. Figure 9.3 presents a possible set of objectives. The involvement of colleagues in discussing the objectives of appraisal may well help to remove the element of threat in the early stages. The opportunity to contribute to the agenda allows for greater understanding of the place which appraisal has in staff development. Also, possible pitfalls can be avoided by an open discussion of the difficulties before implementation.

Appraisal

To conduct an interview annually using the agreed form which is to be signed by both head and colleague and kept for future reference. This procedure will have the following objectives:

To:

1. Assist in self-appraisal of performance.
2. Acknowledge those aspects of work which have proved successful.
3. Assist in the assessment of staff performance and future development.
4. Assist in identification of strengths and weaknesses in the management of the curriculum and classroom organization.
5. Establish realistic agreed objectives.
6. Agree on future action appropriate to the overcoming of difficulties.
7. Agree on courses of action which need to be taken to facilitate colleagues' needs.
8. Assist in decisions involving resource commitments.
9. Help individuals understand the school's organizational needs.
10. Assist in the identification of changes in responsibility as and when appropriate.
11. Discuss a re-evaluation of job specifications.
12. Assist in career development.

N.B. Disciplinary matters have *NO* place in the appraisal interview.

Figure 9.3   A set of objectives for staff appraisal

The appraisal interview and pro forma

Most systems of appraisal used by industry, commerce and the major corporations revolve around the appraisal interview, and the early investigation and resultant research into appraisal in education appears to assume a similar approach. A suitable pro forma will be necessary, both to allow for agreement as to the aspects of the teacher's role which will be discussed, and to

CONFIDENTIAL   ACADEMIC YEAR

TEACHING STAFF – APPRAISAL FORM

NAME......... SCALE......... YEAR GROUP TAUGHT.........

RESPONSIBILITIES (1) .... (2) .... (3) ....

1. PROFESSIONAL ROLE
   (a) PLANNING THE ENVIRONMENT
   Identify how you have:
   (i) designed for the needs of your class and evaluate those policies which have proved successful and those which require further development and/or improvement.
   (ii) planned the organization and management of resources.
   (b) CURRICULUM DEVELOPMENT
   (i) How well have the children responded to the curricular aims and objectives?
   (ii) What aspects of the school's curricular policies have supported or mitigated against the children's development?

2. ADDITIONAL PROFESSIONAL RESPONSIBILITIES
   (i) How relevant is your Job Specification?
   (ii) What changes are appropriate?
   (iii) Which aspects of your role have you concentrated on developing this year?
   (iv) What are your major achievements and what restrictions have you encountered?

3. CAREER DEVELOPMENT
   (i) What are your aspirations for the immediate and long term future?
   (ii) In what ways do you need support to achieve these aspirations?

4. INSET – WHAT COURSES HAVE YOU –
   (i) Attended?
   (ii) Contributed to?
   (iii) What area of your development would benefit from INSET in the immediate future?

5. FURTHER COMMENTS
   Are there any other comments which it has not been possible to include under previous headings?

Date ....   Signed................Teacher

                                       .... Head

Figure 9.4   A specimen pro forma

provide a record as a basis for subsequent appraisals. A specimen pro forma is reproduced as Figure 9.4. Although the format would allow for a directed style of appraisal, the author has used it in a manner consistent with the concept of self-appraisal. During the two weeks prior to the appointed time for the appraisal interview both member of staff and head complete separate forms which become the agenda for the interview, which would normally last for approximately one hour. Following the interview both forms are used by the member of staff who completes a further form which reflects all aspects of the process. Head and member of staff sign the form and it is filed for future reference. Forms should be confidential and ownership lies with head and member of staff.

Appraisal is not an end in itself but a means to an end. It will be severely restricted in value if the process stops with the completion of a form. The benefits will become apparent through planned individual and group development. If measurable benefits do not accrue the appraisal will be a pointless exercise. However, without some system of appraisal, it is difficult to imagine how development can be planned and realistic objectives established.

The appraisal interview requires careful planning. An unstructured, badly planned and interrupted interview is unlikely to achieve anything and may prove to be counterproductive. Detailed planning is important since it is often the apparently trivial which can destroy sensitive moments in a discussion. Allow time to prepare; invest sufficient time to think about the important issues to be addressed. Arrange seating so that it is conducive to discussion; the existence of a desk between appraiser and appraisee not only forms a barrier but may be perceived as a threat. Allow time to talk; the pre-emptory termination of a discussion because another appointment is imminent inevitably leaves the appraisee feeling less important. Try to avoid interruption; this is particularly difficult in school. The telephone can be taken off the hook but some children are unstoppable! The careful planning of the whole process lends credibility to the serious issues which are under discussion.

Appraising the Head

The role of the head

Before any form of appraisal can take place, there must be a clear definition of the role such as is provided by a job specification. Reference was made to this point, earlier in this chapter, with regard to staff appraisal, but the situation is no less applicable to the function of headship. However, the author conducted a piece of research (Moore, 1986) which elicited that, of twenty-six English LEAs which advertised for primary school headteachers in January 1984, only one provided a formal job specification. This situation is substantiated in a forthcoming article by Hellawell. In some current research, on the process of evaluation, he states:

> One of my working hypotheses is that it is very difficult, if not impossible, to appraise someone's performance in a job if the nature of that job is not carefully delineated and there is not a degree of consensus about that delineation. Certainly many large commercial and industrial firms which have had systems of performance appraisal for many years have gone to considerable trouble to analyse what it is that ought to be appraised. A job description, which specifies in great detail the aims and objectives which the postholders are intended to fulfil, are very common in such spheres. From the sample of further particulars which I obtained over this seven-week period it does appear that the jobs of headteachers in primary schools are not, by and large, delineated in such a way at present that their job description could be used as a basis for performance appraisal . . . it has to be stated that job descriptions were, in almost all cases, conspicuous by their absence.
> (Hellawell, 1986, p.1.)

However, the imposition of the Government's *Education (School Teacher's Pay and Conditions of Employment) Order* (1987) which sets a clear, contractual definition of the function of headship, may well bring about rapid change. Clearly the new Order will result in job specifications, which accord with the requirements of the conditions becoming essential, since it is the job specification which defines the responsibilities appropriate to a particular headship. The extent and balance of these responsib-

---

Headteacher – Job Specification

1. To assume responsibility for the internal organization, management and discipline of the school.
2. To act as chief executive and leading professional.
3. To direct policies within a broadly democratic and participative style of leadership.
4. To consult with and report to Governors and LEA.
5. To consult with colleagues as appropriate in:

    (i) Setting the aims, objectives and general ethos of the school.
    (ii) Establishing an environment conducive to the social and educational development of the children.
    (iii) Establishing short- and long-term goals.
    (iv) Selecting, appointing and appraising of staff.
    (v) Dealing with issues relating to boundary management.
    (vi) Communicating with parents.

6. To be involved with children by teaching and taking assemblies, as appropriate, dealing with problems of a disciplinary nature, and handling the procedure for children requiring special needs.
7. To manage the non-teaching staff of the school.
8. The following areas of responsibility are currently delegated to deputy heads.

    (a) (i) Overall co-ordination and development of the curriculum in consultation with curriculum co-ordinators.
       (ii) Children's records.
       (iii) School based INSET.
    (b) (i) Coordination of the administration of the school in consultation with heads of upper, middle and lower school.
       (ii) Communication.
       (iii) Budgeting.

Figure 9.5   A job specification for the headteacher

ilities will vary according to the needs of each individual institution.

The size of a school will, in particular, have implications for the role which a head performs. Issues such as delegation and the extent of any teaching commitment will affect the ways in which the head is able to discharge his functions, especially those with a full-time teaching commitment.

The translation of a definition of the role of headship into a written job specification requires consideration. The head may wish to deal with the matter personally. However, if the role of the head is to be seen in the context of the needs of the school, as outlined early in the chapter, discussion with colleagues may be helpful. The job specification, (Figure 9.5) resulted from extensive consultation between the author and both school deputies. It is not intended as an exemplar but as one school's response to its needs. The discussions also resolved the role of the deputy heads in that the job specifications are subject to annual review and altered as appropriate, in the light of the school's and individual's developmental needs.

The form for the appraisal of the head (Figure 9.6) will need to relate to the job specification and take account of the particular aspects of the head's role. Consideration should also be given as to whether the objectives established for staff appraisal are applicable to the headteacher's appraisal and, if not, the differences should be acknowledged. For example, the existence of objectives relating to teaching performance which might be seen as central to teacher appraisal, may be deemed inappropriate in the case of the head. Given the complexity of the role of the headteacher it may be more valuable to focus on a few aspects of the job specification rather than attempt to cover the entire role superficially.

Who appraises the head?

This question appears to be, at present, a highly controversial issue. The cause of this situation is not clear, and the uncertainty is in contrast to the apparent unanimity expressed by teaching staff that the head is the person who should conduct teacher appraisal. The Suffolk team found that in only two of the schools visited was any attempt made to appraise the head, and in both cases deputy heads did the job. They also found wide ranging alternative suggestions, including the school governors and the

---

Headteacher's Appraisal Form

1. How do you see yourself as a manager, organizer and disciplinarian?
   Strengths:

   Areas for improvement:
2. Staff Development: Priorities for the immediate future?

3. Curriculum Development: What do you see are the successes and what improvements do you see are needed in the immediate future?

4. What are your future plans for the school in terms of aims, objectives and general ethos of the school?

   Organization:

   Community Involvement:

   Parental Involvement:

   Governor Involvement:

   Children with special needs – remedial and very able:

   Internal Communications:

5. Are your school hours utilized to the best advantage for the school?

6. Do you see any areas for improvement in personal relationships?

7. INSET – Courses (i)   attended   (ii)   contributed to
8. Career Development:
   Short term   –   Long term
                          In service needs

Any other points you wish to raise?

Signed ....(Head)
.... (Appraiser)

Figure 9.6   Headteacher's appraisal form

A – Those capable of conducting the appraisal:

  (i)   The deputy head.
  (ii) LEA Inspector/Adviser.
  (iii) A seconded/promoted head.
  (iv) A member of the head's peer group.

B – Those able to contribute to the appraisal:

  (i)   Members of the teaching staff.
  (ii) Members of the non-teaching staff.
  (iii) Governors.
  (iv) Parents.
  (v)   The community.
  (vi) Members of support agencies associated with the school.

Figure 9.7   Who might appraise the headteacher?

head in person. In Somerset, one of the six pilot areas funded by the DES to conduct research into teacher appraisal, early investigation is being carried out on the concept of a '24,000 mile service' whereby each headteacher will be appraised by two heads from a different catchment area in the same authority. The Committee of Heads of Educational Institutions (CHEI), in their proposals for discussion outlined in the journal *Education* of 21 March 1986, suggest that the professional appraisal of headteachers should be conducted by experienced heads of high standing who would serve for a period of one to three years. Turner and Clift (1985) found that some schools had experimented with heads of department, committees of staff and outsiders, (for example from industry) conducting the head's appraisal. Clearly there is much diversity in the early investigative work being carried out and hopefully this may prove productive when guidelines begin to emerge.

When considering the personnel who may be involved with the appraisal process it may be of value to consider two categories; those who might conduct the appraisal and those who could contribute to the appraisal (Figure 9.7). There appear to be three principal criteria by which one might identify the most appropriate people to conduct the appraisal, viz:

1. Expertise in the function of headship.

2. Knowledge of contextual issues relating to the school and its community.
3. Professional acceptability.

Applying these criteria to staff appraisal one would assume, under normal circumstances, that the head would be acceptable on all three aspects. However, when applying the same criteria to the head's appraisal and attempt to match personnel from 'A' in Figure 9.7 we might find, for example, that a deputy head has knowledge of the school and is professionally acceptable but lacks expertise in the function of headship, or that an LEA Inspector possesses the necessary expertise in the function of headship and is professionally acceptable but lacks the necessary detailed knowledge of the school.

The involvement of more than one person to carry out the appraisal interview is one obvious solution. The author's appraisal has been conducted on this basis, following considerable discussion which resulted in the first deputy and the LEA Inspector, with pastoral responsibility for the school, conducting the interview. Both brought relevant expertise, experience and knowledge of the school to the process. The deputy had some ten years experience in that position at the school, including one term spent as acting head. The Inspector had formerly been headteacher of a similar type of school. The deputy head was made the principal appraiser and, during the period leading up to the interview, consulted widely with staff, chairman of the governors and parent governors. In this particular instance the combination of deputy and Inspector has appeared to work well. However, this has been, principally, as a result of the combined expertise of the people involved rather than the positions held, and it is not, therefore, the intention of the author to make a general case for deputy and Inspector to conduct headteachers' appraisal. Other combinations could work equally as well.

Conclusion

The success of any appraisal system will need to be judged on the benefits which accrue, particularly in the quality of the education offered by a school. Appraisal provides an opportunity to make the best use of the most important resource in that provision – the teachers in the schools.

In order to achieve this:

1. Grasp the nettle of headteacher appraisal – the nub of any scheme's credibility is the appraisal of headteachers (Suffolk, 1985).
2. Establish clearly defined, agreed objectives.
3. Consider carefully the contextual importance of inter-personal relationships within the school, particularly with regard to who should be involved in the process.
4. Face difficult situations, when they arise, with openness and honesty.
5. Exclude disciplinary matters from the appraisal interview.
6. Identify the resource implications, particularly that of time.
7. Act on recommendations arising from the appraisal process.
8. Respect sensitive aspects relating to the ownership of forms and confidentiality.

Chapter 10

Classroom Observation

Clive Carthew

Introduction

The model and style of classroom observation described in this chapter are based almost exclusively on a series of practical experiences during the past five years. Each experience has added or confirmed some aspect of the model.

One of my responsibilities as a chief examiner in modern languages for a large examinations board is the annual moderation of assistant examiners. This requires 'sitting-in' as they conduct the examination and then, subsequently, discussing their performance. Two aspects are being appraised – examination technique and assessment accuracy: these are not negotiable. Most people are a little nervous in such a situation, they want to perform well. To reduce this anxiety, to increase the feeling of trust, and to prepare the ground for the next visit, the follow-up discussion contains careful suggestion and considerable praise for what has been done well. A benevolent developmental approach has proved the most constructive, and although there can be no choice about what is to be observed, most examiners look forward to an annual observation to assure them of their growing professional competence.

I have also had an opportunity to work in the classroom with many teachers and lecturers as an advisory teacher. This led to an understanding of the need for genuine negotiation. The work required a responsiveness to what the teacher initiated; it demanded finding out not only what the teacher wanted to deliver and how he or she was intending to deliver it, but also negotiating the role of the advisory teacher in such a context. The valuing of the teacher as an individual and skilled professional, the lack of imposition, and the willingness to take the teacher's starting point as sacrosanct can all conspire to improve dramatically the outcomes of classroom observation.

As a middle manager in a further education college, I failed miserably several years ago at introducing a scheme of classroom observation to a team of full- and part-time lecturers. They simply refused to be involved when I told them of my intention to visit their class. They were quite correct to do so – no declared purpose, no discussion or consultation; result, no observation! Without careful preparation and real participation leading to shared and agreed aims and methods, little will happen.

Such experiences have been augmented by opportunities to learn about various industrial and commercial models of performance appraisal. These models rarely have the equivalent of classroom observation, that is observation of the appraisee 'on-the-job'. They tend to be more 'off-the-job', review dominated models. However, what the more successful models do display are well-planned and well-prepared lead-ups to the review interviews, and equally well-developed follow-up after the interview.

Classroom observation

The majority of practising teachers spend most of their time in the classroom. This is where their influence upon pupils and students is at its most direct and immediate, and where the development of individual children, young people and adults can be affected. This in no way denies or decries the many other activities that make up a teacher's day, week and term, all of which are essential and demanding components for the progress of the school or college, for the department to which the teacher belongs, and for the personal and professional development of the teacher. Indeed, without the discussion, reading, planning, attendance at courses and reflection that are indispensable, the learning experience for pupils and students would be much the poorer. However, such preparation is rather egotistical unless ultimately it is transferred to the benefit of the pupils and students in the teacher's charge, and where the teacher is likely to interact most with the pupil/student – in the classroom.

A classroom, of course, can be just that. It can also be a science, home economics or language laboratory, a workshop or technology area, gymnasium or sports field, music or art room.

Perhaps what it cannot be is an area of the school or college where accidents or *ad hoc* interactions occur – corridors, staffrooms, playgrounds and the like. In other words, it is where 'formal', planned and prepared learning and teaching takes place. To support a teacher in what he or she is trying to do, and to provide relevant and helpful training where appropriate, the observation of performance in such an environment is, then, essential.

If such observation is really to be helpful, then the perception of this aspect of appraisal as being inspectoral, threatening and malevolent has to be altered. One model of classroom observation that may avoid such a negative perception is that based upon negotiation, benevolence and professional development. This model accepts the fact that although more teachers are beginning to be more accustomed to having other teachers in their classrooms, they are still quite anxious about the idea of another person watching their teaching and forming opinions about it. Similarly, many teachers are suspicious that appraisal is concerned with distinguishing shortcomings and faults, and with recording and using them against the teacher.

Negotiation is aimed at overcoming these concerns and anxieties by suggesting that nothing, other than the need for supportive classroom observation, is to be imposed. Thus, the teacher should be encouraged to discuss and agree the timing of any visits, the personnel involved, the sorts of activities to be observed and commented upon, and the final report – if there is to be such a document – including any agreed future actions.

It is equally important that the teacher feels comfortable with the observer. The teacher must have confidence and trust in the person who is watching him or her perform, and feel that benevolent, constructive criticism and practical suggestions will arise as a result of the visit. Benevolence does not mean sycophancy, if it did little progress could be made, and it is this idea of positive progress that should be at the heart of the observation. To support the observation and the ensuing discussion there must be, where appropriate, the possibilities of new opportunities for the teacher who has been observed to progress and develop his or her technique, skills and knowledge and may require off-the-job training and support. They may also be for other teachers who might benefit by hearing or reading about what the 'observed' teacher is doing in a particular area of the curriculum or with an especially successful piece of pedagogical good practice. The main point to keep in mind is that the outcomes of classroom observation should be developmental not absolute; they need to look to the future, to stimulate and encourage both personally and professionally.

The basic questions about classroom observation

Looking more specifically at some of the issues involved in classroom observation and holding firmly to the ideas of negotiation, benevolence and development, two questions immediately arise: 'Who should observe?' and 'What should be observed?' In answer to, 'Who should observe?', the first possibility is, of course, the teacher him or herself. Much of this already occurs, but automatically and subjectively to the point where, in many cases, it has become a reflex action below the level of useful consciousness. If a teacher can devote a little time and effort to a more systematic and objective approach to self-observation then there is, perhaps, much to be gained. At a basic level a teacher may devote 'between-class' time to two questions: either, 'Why did that class go well?' or 'Why did that class go badly?'. This reflective observation can sometimes be quite productive; certainly the more of a habit it becomes, the greater the variety of answers. At a rather more sophisticated level that teacher may deliberately target one class each week for self-observation. During such a session, time has to be set aside to step back from the immediate situation to look at what is happening. Questions such as, 'Am I doing what I intended to do at this point in the class? If not, why not?', and 'Are the pupils/students doing what I hoped they would be doing at this stage? If not, why not?' can be asked and brief answers noted down for later consideration. Involving the pupils/students is more than self-observation but perhaps a little short of peer observation! One way to get a comment from the pupils/students is to ask them at the end of the class to write down briefly what they think has happened in the class, what it was about, what they have learnt or learnt to do, how they have learnt it and how you, the teacher, behaved. If, before looking at what they wrote you write your own answers to the same questions, an interesting comparison of perceptions may throw a little light on how that particular class went.

Peer observation is more demanding in organizational terms and requires greater trust and confidence. In return there is the possibility of benevolent and constructive objectivity at best, and

157

a sympathetic ear at least. Putting aside the logistics, a 'peer' could be from the same school/college, from a different institution, or not from the education service at all. A 'peer' should be a friend or colleague, perhaps someone who teaches the same subject or someone from a completely different discipline or profession. The important thing is that he or she poses no threat, can be trusted to share thoughts only with the teacher and can be relied upon to try to do what is asked. Whereas it is true that nowadays more teachers are more used to having another non-pupil/student in the classroom, it is also true that few teachers are used to this other person watching what is happening and what he or she, the teacher, is doing. It is essential to give some agreed structure and purpose to this observation so that both parties know what is to be done, and what is expected, so that they can subsequently contribute to the ensuing follow-up discussion. Some teachers want a peer observer to concentrate upon their (the teachers) basic delivery – stance, volume, clarity, position in the classroom, etc. – others to look at the use of equipment – OHP, microcomputer, tape recorder – and others to observe how the teacher introduces and maintains groups and group activities. There are obviously many more possibilities but the vital element that links them all is that teacher and observer have agreed beforehand the purpose of the observation and can, therefore, hold a sensible, productive discussion about that issue following the class. The conclusion of such a discussion should be some action – an improvement or innovation aimed at enhancing the pupils'/students' learning experience.

When observation is to be carried out by a superior there is no reason for negotiation, benevolence and a developmental approach to be abandoned. Indeed, it is under such circumstances that these three tenets should be adhered to most firmly. The feeling of inspection must be subordinated to the need for a supportive atmosphere in which the teacher being observed can perform at his or her highest level, and not feel that he or she is about to be caught out or perceived negatively if absolutely everything does not go to plan. Put another way, a superior should be someone that the observed teacher respects and from whom he or she can learn; the observer needs to be someone with greater and wider experience who is capable of commenting constructively on a teacher's performance in a way that promotes a willingness to learn and change. To improve objectivity and perhaps to ensure fairness some people have suggested that a second person ought to be involved with each observation. Three perceptions, it is suggested, are likely to provide a fuller description than two; others suggest that greater arguments would ensue which would not be helpful to the teacher. The cost and time involved would be much heavier, and an implied mistrust of a single observer's skill and experience seems to run counter to the whole idea of negotiation and benevolence.

It is in this last instance, observation by a superior, that the need for observation skills training is essential. In addition to normal interactive personal skills, an observer should also be capable of adjusting his or her approach to the aims and objectives of each individual teacher and class. Following an observation, sensitivity and tact should be used to deliver the appropriate professional descriptions and suggestions.

This brings us to the second question which was, 'What should be observed?' and to the relationship between who and what should be observed. If, for instance, a teacher is anxious to be observed on a new piece of curriculum content, say in mathematics or in French, then it seems reasonable for a mathematics or French teacher to be the observer. If, however, it is the delivery of a piece of curriculum that is to be observed, then maybe it would be better to have a non-specialist as an observer, although certainly in the case of French some knowledge of the language would seem essential. In the case of observation by a superior most teachers would probably look to their head of department/senior lecturer as the appropriate mentor on both content and delivery. Others, however, might want what they would consider to be a more objective viewer and, as discussed above, it is in these situations that the question of content or delivery becomes important. The issue of whether teachers when being observed by a superior should be able to negotiate who carries out the observation is worthy of some debate.

There can be little doubt that most observations will centre upon delivery. This being so, issues of appropriateness, flexibility, variety and successfulness come into play. It can be quite demanding simply to describe what happens in a classroom and even more difficult to make and share opinions about what two people have experienced and perceived. Given the opportunity, then, it can be very helpful to be as specific as possible about what is to be observed. 'Content' and 'delivery' are catch-all words, easily interpreted and intertwined, and they can lead to considerable problems in a post-observation discussion. Some specific classroom activities have been mentioned above; others might come spontaneously from the teacher as items or areas which he or she is finding difficult and with which some guidance or help would be welcome. Some examples might include: use of handouts, control of discussion sessions, working with groups or with one group, use of time, boy/girl bias, and teacher listening skills. To be able to focus the observation to this extent gives real purpose to the event, imposes a tight brief upon the observer and can subsequently provide the teacher with precise support.

A practical model for classroom observation

From the above comments it is possible to describe a practical model for classroom observation which has three distinct sections:

1. Preparatory discussion/interview.
2. Observation.
3. Follow-up discussion/interview leading to agreement on action.

Whether self-observation, peer observation or observation by a superior is being undertaken, the above model is equally applicable. The following comments, however, apply particularly to observation by a superior.

A. Preparatory discussion/interview

A sensible amount of time should be allocated to this activity and a reasonably private and comfortable environment used. The time should be used:

1. To establish, if necessary, some relationship and rapport.
2. To clarify the purpose of the observation.
3. To agree mutually convenient dates for both the observation and the follow-up discussion.
4. To agree the general aim of the follow-up discussion.
5. To establish the nature of the class to be observed.
6. To establish its position in relation to the teacher's scheme of work or syllabus.
7. To establish the aim and objective(s) of the learning/ teaching to be undertaken in the class.

8. To establish the specific aim of the observation.
9. To agree on the introduction of the observer to the class, where he or she will initially or continuously sit, and whether he or she will say anything during the class.

B. Observation

This should take place as and when agreed, unless it is impossible so to do. A considerable amount of preparation by both teacher and observer should have gone into this activity, with the target of a particular class. If for any reason the observation of that class cannot take place, then in all fairness both teacher and observer should return to section A and start again.

C. Follow-up discussion/interview leading to agreement on action

Comments about time and place are the same as those for the preparatory discussion/interview.

1. The aim of the follow-up should be reiterated.
2. The area of the discussion should be that agreed upon in the preparatory session.
3. A genuine discussion should be expected to take place.
4. Some agreed action should arise.
5. Agreement should be reached on any written statement of the observation.

Several issues arise from such a model. Three are discussed below:

(i) However well negotiated the observation and however benevolent and developmental in approach both the observer and the teacher aim to be, there are bound to be occasional disagreements. These can arise from different perceptions or interpretations and can quickly polarize into unproductive static positions. Some method of arbitration and moderation must be available to deal with such situations which maintains both the value of observation and the right of the teacher to ask for 'a second opinion'. It is to be hoped that with sensitivity, benevolence and careful preparation such disagreements will be kept to an absolute minimum. If not, the credibility of the whole idea is called into question.

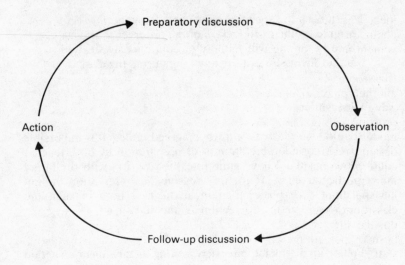

Figure 10.1   Classroom observation as a developmental process

(ii)   The model has considerable resource implications, more so if one believes that a one-off observation of each teacher might hardly provide an honest view of him or her. Repeated or multiple observations will clearly be more productive and representative, but even more time consuming. They will also make the model a more on-going and developmental process.

In such a rolling programme the teacher and observer can target specific areas for action after the first follow-up discussion and can see these at work in the second observation.

The timing of any observation can also be important, as it may be quite different to observe a teacher at the beginning of a new session, with a new class, rather than in the middle or at the end of a session when a changed and perhaps more relaxed and trusting relationship might considerably affect the style and method of delivery.

(iii)   In a school or college where such a model was adopted there would clearly be a need for some system of management and control. Unmanaged, haphazard arrangements would obviously lead to a variety of stresses, tensions and clashes which could quite quickly cause a detrimental wash-back on the whole idea. The need to manage a system leads to further questions about the personnel involved, planning, whole-instruction involvement and the confidentiality of records.

Classroom observation for many teachers is a new idea and is yet another piece of change. To reduce resistance to this change, ways and means have to be found to prove the benefits of such a process. To say that it has to happen, to impose a rigid top-down model will be unproductive, whereas to involve teachers in the design and development of their own schemes of observation could prove much more helpful. Looking for a starting point, or more precisely a starting person, may require the identification of key personnel, one or two teachers who would look upon classroom observation as an opportunity to show what they can do. To involve such people in the early stages can lead to a positive perception of the idea by many other less convinced staff.

Another strategy implied earlier in this chapter is to introduce classroom observation in stages:

1. Self observation
2. Peer observation
3. Observation by a superior

One advantage of such a progression is that many, if not all, teachers should have the opportunity, through peer observation, to take on the role of observer. In this way the teacher can experience the demands, difficulties and limitations of observing before being involved him or herself in a more formal observation by a superior. An opportunity like this may reinforce in each teacher's mind that there are many different and successful ways of teaching, all valid. It might also reinforce the need to discover, through discussion and negotiation, where the teacher to be observed is, in the sense of his or her experience, confidence and professional maturity: assuming that the teacher to be observed is where the observer would like or expect him or her to be does not suggest benevolent negotiation. This role reversal, then, can be quite a productive activity for all participants.

Finally, it is the responsibility of those introducing any scheme of classroom observation to convince all taking part that the exercise is one which is concerned with improving on-the-job teaching skills to enhance both the job satisfaction of the teacher and the learning experiences of the pupils and students.

Chapter 11

Staff Appraisal and the Professional Development of Teachers

Les Bell

Approaching staff appraisal

This book has documented some of the ways in which staff appraisal has been approached in schools. It has not tried to provide a comprehensive analysis of all the issues which are raised by the introduction of appraisal but it has dealt with many of the more significant ones by showing how they were dealt with in practice. Most of the key questions about staff appraisal have been touched upon, including who should appraise whom, when and where, and what are the available forms of appraisal? Various models have been suggested but the most significant factor which emerges when exploring such questions is that if a system of staff appraisal is to be adopted in any school then it should be derived from and be compatible with the particular circumstances of that school. It should not be imposed from outside or be based on inappropriate approaches transplanted unthinkingly from elsewhere. Ideas developed by others can be used, hence the purpose of this book, but these should be modified and adapted to suit each individual school.

We do not present staff appraisal as 'the alchemy for turning base metal teachers into golden ones' (Bunnell and Stephens, 1984, p.291) or the mechanism by which the incompetent can be removed and the capable promoted more rapidly. The main question which has been addressed by all the contributors is how can staff appraisal contribute to more effective professional development of teachers? The position taken by most of the contributors has been, 'If we want an appraisal scheme to match our needs and principles we must involve ourselves in the making of it.' (Bunnell and Stephens, 1984, p.291.) Evaluation of our own performance is a corporate professional exercise and, therefore, we must all involve ourselves in the processes which contribute to it. Such involvement has to include participation in the discussions which precede the introduction of the process and consultation about the nature of the process. C.D.M. Rhodes, Clive Carthew, Jenny Morris and S.M. Slater all make this point forcefully as it is only in this way that staff appraisal can be seen to be truly formative rather than summative. Only formative staff appraisal can be concerned with the professional development of teachers. Richardson gives us a detailed account of how this process evolved in his school, while Harry Moore gives us a different but equally relevant insight into a similar process.

Some of the significant features of the staff appraisal schemes considered here include the extent to which they all provided opportunities for the appraisee to explore his or her own staff development needs based on an open discussion of performance within the context of what the school or the department had been trying to achieve. Opportunities have also been provided to explore the extent to which improvement is thought by both parties to be necessary in any particular area, and to attempt to identify appropriate career changes or developments which may need to take place in order to maximize the individual's career potential. On the basis of this, actions can be agreed to bring about these improvements, developments and changes. It is, then, the responsibility of the appraiser to ensure that the necessary resources are provided in order that these agreed targets can be met. The appraisal interview can be extended to cover the ambitions and aspirations of individuals and their potential for taking on more demanding jobs. It may also be that views and feelings about the job, the department, or the school emerge and these may be as useful to the appraiser as to the appraisee. In short, successful staff appraisal in schools can lead to the exploration and clarification of a number of points for both the individual and the school. These may take the form of questions which, while they would not be the focus of the content of the staff appraisal interview nor the preparation for it, would be explored indirectly during the interview. Questions such as these are implicit in the approach adopted by both S.M. Slater and A.J. Richardson in their different schools. The exploration of issues such as these lead to the individual having a clearer understanding of what his or her role is in the school, what the expectations of other people of him or her are, and lead to a better understanding of how he or she is fulfilling those expectations.

QUESTIONS	QUESTIONS
For the individual	**For the School**
Who is my BOSS? What is my JOB? HOW am I doing? WHAT am I doing well? How can I do BETTER?	Policy making • Who does what? • when? • with what? • to whom?
	Implementation • How are tasks delegated?
How do I see the organisation helping me?	• What are the principles? • How is co-ordination carried out?
	Monitoring and Evaluation • Are tasks being carried out? • How well? • What needs change? • Are results being achieved?
	Policy Revision • What needs changing? • By whom? • By when? • How?

Figure 11.1   Questions explored by appraisal process

(Derived from a lecture given by Dr Patrick Bailey at the University of Leicester School of Education to an NDC/SMT Conference on Staff Appraisal, 14.11.85, quoted in Bell and Arnold [1987]).

A similar perspective can be found in *School Evaluation*, where it is argued that:

> If staff are to be encouraged or required to give of their best then opportunities must exist to provide discussion about their performance in relation to expectations. Staff must then receive feedback on both expectations and performance. Teachers then have a right to know:
>
> (a)   To whom am I responsible?
> (b)   For what am I responsible?
> (c)   What am I expected to do?
> (d)   How am I doing?
> (e)   How can I do my job better?
>
> Teachers also have the right to have access to anything that is written about them and the right to respond or appeal. They have a right to expect a negotiated programme of professional development. Employers and those in authority also have a right to show what is going on in school/sections and a right to expect teachers to develop and expand their skills through professional development.
> (Solihull, 1986, p.29).

Obviously, the introduction of staff appraisal into any school requires thorough preparation, careful planning and a high degree of sensitivity. The success of any appraisal system in any school depends to a large extent on the willingness of all members of the organization to give their commitment to that process. There will be teething problems, difficulties, and anomalies but the advantages and benefits both to the school and to individual teachers can be considerable. It is teachers' careers that are under discussion. This requires an exercise of judgement and care. As appraisees we have to be receptive and cooperative, seeing the benefits to ourselves and the needs of the school. As appraisers we have to weigh our words like responsible critics and be aware of their possible effects. We have a chance to show appreciation, to learn and to help. We must focus as much as humanly possible on the positive and the good while seeking to improve and develop rather than to criticize and blame. Appraisal provides us all with an opportunity to make the best use of the most important resource we have in our schools, our colleagues.

Staff appraisal: problems and possibilities

Even in the most positive of climates the introduction of staff appraisal to schools brings disadvantages as well as advantages. Bell and Arnold (1987) point out that although appraisal may be based on the provision of opportunities for professional development, the major disadvantage associated with its introduction is the fact that it will require a significant amount of scarce resources devoted to it in terms of time and of money. It may be unrealistic to expect an appraisal process to be carried out outside normal working hours. Therefore, the resources have to be provided in order to free those people who are involved in the process so that they can meet, prepare for, and conduct appraisal interviews, and also that they can follow up the interviews effectively. Resources will also be required in order to meet the training needs which such a process undoubtedly identifies. Wilcox (1986) has suggested that the introduction of a systematic appraisal system into all schools will require:

1. Central administration.
2. Release time for all teachers.
3. Training for heads, deputies, and heads of departments.
4. Secretarial costs.

He argued that this could cost LEAs £900,000 in one year. These costs do not include the meeting of the subsequent training needs either in school or from the resources of the LEA. Such additional costs are too complicated to be able to compute with any degree of accuracy given that the funding on in-service training is undergoing a radical change. Apart from the cost in resource terms the other major disadvantage associated with the introduction of staff appraisal into schools is the cost in personal terms. An effective process requires honesty and courage in its application to all colleagues. It requires objectivity and the ability to separate personal relationships from professional relationships. It also requires those involved to recognize that appraisal can provoke conflict and controversy, but that it need not do so if those involved are well trained and are committed to carrying out the process effectively.

Other disadvantages associated with appraisal often reflect a set of assumptions about the meanings attached to appraisal by those people who are in favour of its introduction into schools. It was argued in chapter 1 that there are those who are concerned appraisal would be used as a form of redeployment, as a technique for eliminating rather than helping weak teachers, or as a management tool to restructure the school without adequate consultation. These fears have led to the development of an argument in favour of 'appraisal from below'. This may have some limited value in that it permits a change of ideas and enables the senior member of the school to appreciate the impact of his or her actions on more junior colleagues. It has to be recognized, however, that there will be many aspects of, say, the role of the head of department, about which a junior member of that department is entirely unaware and, therefore, would be unable to comment upon in a meaningful or helpful way. An effective appraisal process should enable colleagues to explore the extent to which their professional relationship is an effective one and to seek ways of improving the quality of that relationship.

When the potential benefits of staff appraisal are considered, Bell and Arnold (1987) suggest that it provides the opportunity for identifying and appraising good performance and encouraging improved performance. A number of general benefits can, therefore, be identified including the extent to which staff appraisal would help schools in the process of curriculum development, in-service training, problem solving, increased motivation and more public credibility for teachers. More specifically, however, they argue, that a systematic process of staff appraisal would encourage schools to be much clearer and more specific about their overall aims, their objectives, and their strategies for achieving these. Such a process would also require that teachers have a clear and thorough understanding of what their total responsibilities are: how they are expected to carry them out and the extent to which they have been successful. Thus the school will benefit from a better overall understanding of how teachers see their jobs, how satisfied they are with them, and what changes, if any, staff wish to make. This, then, provides an opportunity to enable schools to plan for major and minor changes in all areas and to ensure that staff development and training can be related both to this and to the strengthening of those aspects of the school's work in which improvements in performance may be necessary. Appraisal provides for the school an opportunity to plan and make the best use of the available potential and abilities within the staff team. It can also help to develop an ethos within which major educational and professional issues are depersonalized in such a way that honest communication and understanding can take place between committed professionals without the petty personal wrangles which sometimes accompany this process. Relationships may, therefore, be improved within the school.

More generally, however, a systematic process of staff appraisal is an open process and can be seen to be such. This reduces, although it cannot entirely eliminate, the subjectivity from the professional assessment of the work of colleagues. It does provide a permanent, shared, and agreed set of records upon which to base the discussion of the work of any individual teacher within the specific context of the school, the department, or the duties and responsibilities of the post held by that individual. It can also provide a much fairer and more up-to-date basis for making professional judgements, which, at times, we are all required to make about our colleagues when they are seeking promotion or other forms of career enhancement. If the process is carried out effectively, the person being appraised has as much ownership of the process and its outcomes as the person carrying out the appraisal. This can, in the right circumstances, increase motivation and improve morale since each individual within the school gains a greater sense of belonging through realization of the value of his or her contribution to the school and the recognition that the individual's professional development is a significant part of the concerns of the school.

If appraisal can help schools to be clearer about their aims and objectives it can also lead to the clarification of personal roles and responsibilities within the school and provide for the individual to receive a relatively objective assessment of his or her performance related to a set of plans for improving, developing, or changing the professional competencies of that teacher where it can be agreed that this is necessary. The teacher receives help and encouragement to develop in appropriate ways, and is able to play a significant part in the process of identifying his or her own staff development needs. Thus we do not wish to suggest that the introduction of staff appraisal in schools is without problems or difficulties. In fact staff appraisal has associated with it a range of disadvantages which may counter-balance its advantages. It is the experience of most of the contributors to this book that the advantages outweigh the disadvantages and the more closely linked appraisal is to staff development (see Figure 11.2) the more likely this is to be the case.

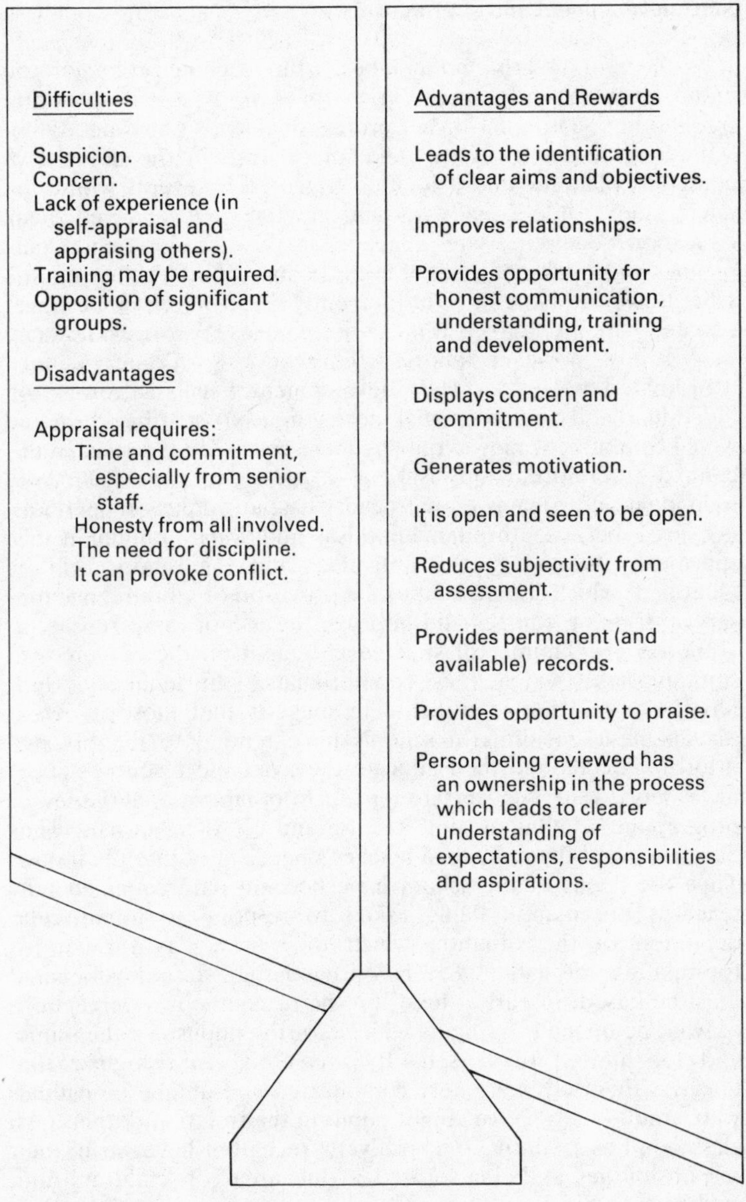

Difficulties

Suspicion.
Concern.
Lack of experience (in
    self-appraisal and
    appraising others).
Training may be required.
Opposition of significant
    groups.

Disadvantages

Appraisal requires:
    Time and commitment,
        especially from senior
        staff.
    Honesty from all involved.
    The need for discipline.
    It can provoke conflict.

Advantages and Rewards

Leads to the identification
    of clear aims and objectives.

Improves relationships.

Provides opportunity for
    honest communication,
    understanding, training
    and development.

Displays concern and
    commitment.

Generates motivation.

It is open and seen to be open.

Reduces subjectivity from
    assessment.

Provides permanent (and
    available) records.

Provides opportunity to praise.

Person being reviewed has
    an ownership in the process
    which leads to clearer
    understanding of
    expectations, responsibilities
    and aspirations.

Figure 11.2   Staff appraisal in the balance

Les Bell

Staff development and staff appraisal

It has been argued that no member of the teaching profession can enter teaching and remain in it for several decades without frequently updating his or her professional skills (AMMA, 1985). Although development can take place even in the absence of conscious planning and it is often triggered by events within the environment, it is equally certain that the rapid changes facing education today indicate a need for this development to be planned in a systematic way if both the individual teacher and the school are to benefit. Until recently 'staff-development' was equated with attendance at in-service courses. We would contend there is now, however, a need within schools for a clearly defined coordinated policy for staff development which satisfies both individual and organizational needs in a compatible way and which cannot be achieved only by mere course attendance. In this context, therefore, 'appraisal', as a means of identifying both individual and organizational needs, has advantages for schools, not least because through appraisal additional training needs, specifically related to the individual and the school, will be identified, which should lead to the provision of more relevant in-service training courses and improve the use of these resources.

Basing programmes of staff development on the outcomes of staff appraisal will help to counterbalance the tendency which Shipton (1987) has identified. He suggests that those in senior management positions in schools have tended to identify and prioritize needs and then allocate the available resources. They have tended to concentrate on such organizational issues as programme scheduling, time release and use of resources. They have expected the individual teacher's needs to fit into the model. Thus the needs of the school have become paramount and the teachers are merely being asked to respond to a particular definition of the situation which they may play no part in formulating. Gough (1985) has argued that staff development must be based, in part at least, on the teacher's own perceptions of what he or she is trying to achieve for the pupils, for the school and for himself or herself. It is essential to recognize that teachers themselves are very complicated and unique individuals who, traditionally, have taught pupils in the isolation of their own classroom and, until comparatively recently, have seen their responsibilities as being located in the areas of 'children' and, perhaps, 'subject'. Teachers have, of course, turned to their colleagues for help, support and advice. As Nias (1984) makes us aware, it is through factors like isolation, self-reliance, autonomy and individualism that teachers construct their own 'ideal' model of a teacher from chance encounters, inference and imagination. She argues that staff development initiatives should acknowledge both the isolating nature of classroom teaching and the rooted individualism of teachers, since it appears that teachers do have a strong sense of personal and professional identity. Thus there may be a conflict between the individual staff development needs, as perceived by each individual teacher, and the needs of the school in relation to broader aspects of school policy and school development in terms both of direction and priorities. It can be seen from several of the contributions to this book, notably Jenny Morris, A.J. Richardson and S.M. Slater, that staff appraisal provides one way to balance the needs of the individual and the needs of the school. It at least enables plans for staff development to be based on accurate information. At the same time, however, it remains important to stress that staff appraisal and self-evaluation are both part of an individual teacher's personal professional development.

If the prime purpose of staff appraisal is to improve the quality and organization of teaching and learning in schools, then as Nisbet argues, appraisal:

> . . . should be beneficial in its effect. It should be linked to a development programme which will provide support to improve staff performance. It must not damage or distort the processes of learning and teaching. It must not damage morale, destroy relationships and trust . . . It should be fair. It must not only operate equitably for all concerned, but also be seen as working fairly . . . It should be comprehensive, covering the full range of work done by teachers. . . It should be valid . . . (Nisbet, 1986, p.16.)

Nisbet's criteria for effective and acceptable processes have been developed further by Nuttall (1986) who identifies a number of such qualities. Firstly is the need for trust among the staff and commitment from the top which, together, can facilitate a climate of constructive self-criticism. Secondly is the requirement that formative and summative purposes should not be undertaken simultaneously or by the same set of processes. Thirdly, the outcomes of the process should be linked to appropriate actions, the resources for which must be forthcoming. Fourthly is the importance of involving those who will be appraised in the development of the scheme rather than imposing it upon them.

This must, in turn, result in effective self-appraisal becoming an important component, although not the only one, in the appraisal process. Fifthly, Nuttall argues, an acceptable scheme must give the teachers some autonomy and provide them with some control over the process. Similarly, Warwick (1983) has suggested among the criteria that effective appraisal must meet are the following:

1. It must be accepted both by those having been appraised and those appraising.
2. It must be open.
3. It must be comprehensive.
4. It must involve self assessment.
5. It must be consistent.
6. It must be planned.

Trethowan, emphasizing the role of target setting in the appraisal process, has argued that the main purpose of appraisal is the improvement of performance, which, in turn, should lead to continuous supportive development (Trethowan, 1987, p.73). In order to achieve this he suggests job descriptions, a clearly defined set of management responsibilities, appropriate documentation, and well conducted appraisal interviews will all be required. Most of the studies of staff in this volume highlight similar issues. All emphasize the need for trust, openness and the need for consultation and planning, although Francis Arnold shows that not all of the staff of any one school need to be involved in the first instance. A.J. Richardson and C.D.M. Rhodes make a similar point while the importance of a well conducted interview is recognized by everyone. Jenny Morris shows how staff appraisal and the information obtained from it can be used to form and reform groups of teachers based on their interests and enthusiasms, thus making more effective use of staff while, at the same time, providing them with greater job satisfaction.

If, then, the main purpose of staff appraisal is to promote the most effective deployment of teachers and to ensure that teachers have access to coherent, relevant programmes of staff development, in order that pupils in schools may receive the maximum benefit from their education, then it must be recognized that any formal review is only part of a continuous process of monitoring and evaluation. This on-going assessment will include regular and *ad hoc* meetings and discussions about objectives, performance and staff development (Bell and Arnold, 1987). If assessment is continuous it should point to difficulties and shortcomings as they emerge, and not produce them as some diabolic behavioural rabbit from the appraiser's hat. The appraisal meeting, by its deliberate formality, points to the importance of the whole appraisal exercise. It is the bringing together of reviewer and reviewee in a discussion which embraces successes, aspirations, frustrations, problems and needs which can influence performance and development. Very few people are prepared to operate in a state of vacuum of assumption – assumption that their job performance is completely acceptable and that their individual concerns, aspirations and hopes are known. It is incomprehensible that schools have tended to operate on the basis of 'I'll soon let you know if you're doing something wrong' but this approach is more prevalent than one might imagine and the fault is often compounded by reference or criticism made of which the person concerned is not aware. Appreciation and praise, comment and criticism should be open and fully explored. This is the key for any honest relationship between people. Within the context of any appraisal system it is absolutely essential and must be viewed as the core principle. Any form of reviewing, reporting or appraisal scheme which does not provide for the subject to be aware (by seeing what has been written) and does not allow discussion and appeal is suspect and open to abuse. It must be appreciated, however, that pure objectivity is unattainable, and self-awareness will always be clouded by self-perception. It is important to remember that, as Miles (1984) points out, staff appraisal should never become a substitute for the regular discussion between colleagues which should always be taking place. Nor should it be conducted or documented in an inappropriately bureaucratic way that may damage the professional relationship upon which teaching hitherto, has been based. Thus:

> What we should be looking for is not a slavish copy of an
> outdated industrial model, but something . . . distinctive,
> capable of providing its own challenge . . .
> (Miles, 1984, p.236.)

In order to do this the appraisal of individual teachers needs to be closely related to the aims of their schools and the strategies for the school's future development. Thus there needs to be a clear understanding by all participants as to how the processes of staff appraisal and the criteria adopted relate to the basic aims of the school. There also needs to be an agreement that the appraisal process reflects and considers the most important aspects of the work of the school.

175

Staff appraisal and school development

One way to achieve this is to develop an appraisal process which is closely linked to the overall aims and objectives of the school, very much as S.M. Slater has done at Park Hall. As both Warwick (1983) and Nutall (1986) have pointed out, there is a need within the school for a climate that allows for open discussion, negotiation, trust, respect, and ownership of collaborative processes. The achievement of such a climate is, however, dependent on a number of factors and it is important to recognize and take into account the current stage of development of the school in deciding the time scale of the activities. (See Figure 11.3)

The management of the introduction of the concept of staff appraisal needs into the school is fundamental to ultimate success. Two elements are seen as particularly crucial in this introduction:

1. Openness and clear communication.
2. The need for staff to take ownership of the process in such a way as to ensure that it is shared dialogue between colleagues which can be conducted on the basis of mutual trust and respect.

In some schools, this may be done by arranging a meeting where the whole staff can discuss the need for, and issues related to, appraisal. In other schools the existing discussion/communication structures may be used if appropriate. Such ways of consulting the staff may include whole-staff meetings, departmental meetings and meetings of existing committees. It may be desirable to use more than one of these, for example, a meeting of senior staff, followed by a full staff meeting and developed further in departmental or other meetings. The next stage could be for the headteacher to nominate a teacher with responsibility for staff development and staff appraisal and to manage a professional development group which would be representative of the staff as a whole. In smaller schools this may well be the whole staff. All colleagues will need to be well briefed about the purpose of the activity and about the processes to be used in order to carry out individual staff appraisals and to relate these to the needs of the school as well as to a coherent programme of staff development.

The staff appraisal interview will be central to the process. This should be a helping activity based on open communication and owned jointly by the parties involved as Francis Arnold and A.J.

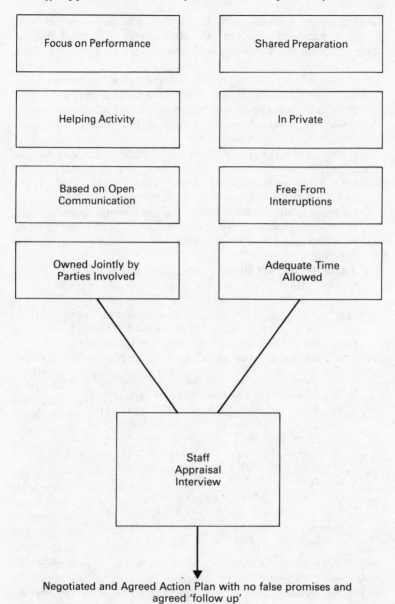

Figure 11.3   Key elements in the staff appraisal interview

Les Bell

Richardson have shown in their chapters. The interview, as both Kingsley Bungard and C.D.M. Rhodes have pointed out, is carried out on the following basic principles:

1. It should be conducted on the basis of a genuine two-way professional exchange and should concentrate on the present circumstances and future developments. The discussion should, however, ensure that the teacher's contribution plays a major part.
2. It should produce a negotiated and agreed action with no false promises.
3. It should be related directly to the role which the individual plays in the school. It should seek to achieve a congruence between the individual's needs and those of the school. It should also consider the teacher's future aspirations and identify areas for possible future development.
4. There should be a structure to the discussion and this structure should be understood/agreed by all the parties to the process who should be able to prepare themselves in advance. This is essential to ensure self-awareness and maximum value to the teacher concerned. This preparation which would help focus the discussion could take a variety of forms including for example:

   • A key activity list for the individual's particular role.
   • Consideration of the teacher's job description.
     The job description itself may form part of the exchange. For example, one useful element of the discussion may be the extent to which the teacher's perception of his or her job description matches the 'official' or 'formal' job description. This may lead to a negotiation of a change in the job description as part of the identification of needs process.
   • A check-list or questionnaire completed by individual teachers indicating their own strengths and development needs.

The interview should focus on agreed areas of performance and time must be allowed for both parties to prepare fully.

The 'interviewer' may be the headteacher or other member of the senior management team. Personality rather than position is, however, seen as crucial, with trust and empathy being particularly highlighted. However, if not the headteacher, the

178

'interviewer' must be provided with clearly defined areas of responsibility and the parameters of his or her decision making. It is important that the discussions should be in private, free from interruptions and with adequate time allowed. The outcome of the interview should be an agreement in the form of an individual staff development plan for the teacher involved in the professional exchange. This will be confidential to the parties involved and to those in the school who are responsible for meeting the professional development needs of colleagues. The initial discussion may result in follow-up interviews, by agreement between those involved in the initial exchange, if further attention is required in specific specialist areas. How, then, can staff appraisal be limited to both individual and school development needs in such a way as to emphasize the formative aspects of staff appraisal and to eliminate the summative elements? A number of possible models suggest themselves. For example, Jenny Morris in her role as professional tutor developed an approach which helped staff to understand more fully the philosophy and objectives of a newly amalgamated school. The interviews here seemed almost therapeutic at times. S.M. Slater, in his first school developed a model based on discussions involving all the staff. This took the aims and objectives of each department as its starting point. In his present school he has adopted a similar process through a series of in-service training days. Here the starting focus is the whole school's aims and objectives and the existing management structure provides the framework for the process. A.J. Richardson based his approach on the professional concerns of his staff.

A similar approach to that of Slater and Richardson, which is also based on detailed discussions with staff about the objectives of the school, its organizational needs, and the professional development needs of the staff, is illustrated in Figure 11.4. Here full consideration of the needs of the school take place in parallel with the introduction of staff appraisal so that discussions in one area can inform those in another. Simply described, the process might begin with a whole-staff consultation, out of which a group responsible for managing the process would be identified. Most schools, as a result of GRIST, already have a staff-development coodinator who should be involved in the process. If a supporting group of colleagues can be identified the ownership of the process can be more widely shared and, when appraisal interviews are being considered, a number of this group might be involved where appropriate. As a result of discussion at school,

179

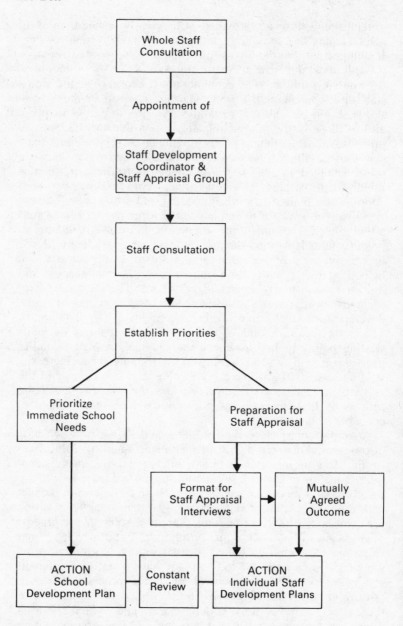

Figure 11.4   School development and staff appraisal

department or other functional group level, the main priorities for the school might be identified and agreed upon before appraisal interviews start. In this way the action plans, which will result from the appraisal interviews, can be informed by the discussions on the school's immediate needs. The professional development of individual teachers can, in this way, be more closely linked to the priorities of the school. In turn, this will make it more likely that those needs can and will be met. The meeting of individual staff development needs as they emerge from the appraisal process is, perhaps, the single most important factor in ensuring that staff appraisal is successful in so far as it is understood and accepted by teachers and it produces the desired outcomes for their pupils – that is, an improvement in the quality of the education which they receive. It must always be recognized that the principal aim of teacher appraisal should be the improvement of children's education.

Notes on contributors

Francis Arnold is a management consultant working in the public and private sectors. He works with the Church, the Police and several national and international companies. Over a third of his work involves him in the education sector with schools, colleges of further education, LEAs and Universities. He is particularly interested in managing change, team development and staff appraisal and has published many articles on management training and development.

Les Bell taught in both primary and secondary schools before entering teacher education. He joined the University of Warwick on 1 April 1978 when Coventry College of Education was merged with it. He is now a Senior Lecturer in Education in the DES and has special responsibility for courses in educational management. He has acted as a consultant on educational management for a large number of schools and LEAs and has written extensively on school organization and management.

Kingsley Bungard obtained a Diploma in Management Studies and a PGCE before becoming a Lecturer in Business Management at Kent College of Further Education. Subsequently he has been an industrial training advisor and the manager of a Management Training Centre. He is now Director of Professional Development at Silsoe College, Cranfield Institute of Technology. He has worked extensively in management training for heads and teachers in schools, especially in the areas of staff appraisal and staff development.

Clive Carthew has a background in modern languages. He became a Senior Lecturer in the Management and Business Studies Department of a further education college and a chief examiner for the Associated Examining Board. He has recently been working as a TRIST advisory teacher and, in September 1987, he joined the West Midlands Examining Board as Principal Assistant Secretary. He has two text books published by Longman and is presently preparing a book on educational management.

Harry Moore has been a headteacher for fourteen years. Since 1980 he has been head of a group 7 Primary School with a Nursery Unit. His introduction of staff appraisal to this school is part of a research project being carried out by the Open University. He has been involved in management courses at the Open University, Birmingham Polytechnic and the University of Warwick.

Jenny Morris trained as an English teacher and was a head of department before becoming a deputy headteacher of a high school in Rugby. This school was closed in 1985 and its staff and pupils were amalgamated with two other schools to form the new Ashlawn School. She is now one of the deputy headteachers of the new school. Her duties include a responsibility for staff development. Her other interests include multi-racial and multi-cultural education, community relations and the Young Enterprise Scheme.

Chris Rhodes worked for the Service Children's Education Authority for thirteen years and has experienced formal teacher appraisal with that authority which introduced it in the late 1970s. Since 1980 he has been head of Sydenham County Middle School, Leamington Spa and regularly contributes to management courses.

Tony Richardson taught in a number of primary schools before becoming head of Green Lanes Primary School, Metropolitan Borough of Solihull in 1984. He has contributed extensively to in-service courses, especially in the areas of educational drama and approaches to pupil personal development in the primary school, and he has published a number of articles. His school has received a grant from SCDC to develop pupil autonomy in Learning.

183

ERRATUM

P. 182 — Les Bell is now Senior Lecturer in the Education Department at the University of Warwick

Sid Slater   is the head of Park Hall School in the Metropolitan Borough of Solihull before which he was head of Abraham Moss High School in Manchester, and Assistant Principal of the North Manchester College. He is editor of the *Journal of Evaluation in Education* and has published widely on school evaluation, staff appraisal, links between education and industry and curriculum innovation. He has also directed a large number of regional and national conferences on school evaluation.

Norman Thomas   was a primary schoolteacher and headteacher before joining HM Inspectorate in 1962. He retired from HMI in 1982 as Chief Inspector for Primary and Middle Schools. Since then he has continued writing and lecturing on educational matters, chairing the committee of inquiry into primary education in ILEA. *Improving Primary Schools* (1985), acting as specialist adviser to the House of Commons, Education, Science and Arts Committee in its inquiry into primary education.

Bibliography

Adams, D. *Life, the Universe and Everything*, Barker, 1982.

Alexander, R. *Primary Teaching*, Holt Education, 1984.

Assistant Masters and Mistresses Association. *Appraisal: Trick or Treat? An AMMA discussion document*, AMMA, 1985.

Bell, L.A. 'Appraisal and Schools' in *Management in Education*, Volume 1, Number 1, 1987, pp.30–34.

Bell, L.A. and Arnold, F. 'Introducing Staff Appraisal to Schools' in *School Organisation*, Volume 7, Number 2, 1987, pp.193–207.

Bell, L.A. and Maher, P. *Leading a Pastoral Team. A Staff Development Approach*, Blackwells, 1986.

Bell, L.A. *'Teacher Attitudes to Appraisal: a survey of conference members*, University of Warwick, DES Mimeo, 1985.

Blackburn, K. 'Teacher Appraisal' in M. Marland (Ed.) *School Management Skills*, Heinemann Organisation in Schools Series, 1986.

Bunnell, S. and Stephens, E. 'Teacher Appraisal – A Democratic Approach' in *School Organisation*, Volume 4, Number 4, 1984, pp.291–302.

Butterworth, I.B. *The Appraisal of Teachers*, Educational Management Information Exchange Paper, 1985.

Campbell, R.J. *Developing the Primary Curriculum*, Holt, Rinehart & Winston, 1985.

Clift, P. 'LEA Schemes for School Self-Evaluation' in *Educational Research*, Volume 24, Number 4, pp.26–35.

Croydon LEA. *A System of Professional Performance Appraisal Discussion Document*, London Borough of Croydon, 1984.

Cumbria LEA. *The Appraisal and Professional Development of Teaching Staff*, Cumbria Education Committee, 1985.

Day, C., Johnstone, D. and Whitaker, P. *Managing Primary Schools*, Harper & Row, 1986.

Day, C. and Moore, R. *Staff Development in The Secondary School*, Croom Helm, 1987.

Bibliography

Dean, J. 'Teacher Appraisal: some questions to ask' in *Inspection and Advice*, Volume 22, Number 1, 1986.

Delaney, P. 'Teacher appraisal in the Primary School: One School's Experience.' *Junior Education Special Report*, Scholastic Publication, 1986.

DES, (1972). *Teacher Education and Training, (The James Report)*, HMSO.

DES, (1979a). *Aspects of Secondary Education in England*, HMSO.

DES, (1979b). *A Framework for the School Curriculum*, HMSO.

DES, (1981a). *The School Curriculum*, HMSO.

DES, (1981b). *Circular 6.81*, HMSO.

DES, (1983). *Teaching Quality*, HMSO.

DES, (1985a). *Better Schools*, HMSO.

DES, (1985b). *Quality in Schools: Evaluation and Appraisal*, HMSO.

DES, (1985c). *The Curriculum from 5 to 16: Curriculum Matters 2*, HMSO.

DES, (1987). *The Education Act*, HMSO.

DES, (1986). *The Education (School Teachers' Pay and Conditions of Employment) Order*, HMSO.

Des Forges, B. 'Staff development, assessment and evaluation' *Review: Secondary Headteacher's Association*, Volume 79, December, 1984.

Dockrell, B., Nisbet, J., Nuttall, D., Stones, E, and Wilcot, B. *Appraising Appraisal*, British Educational Research Association, 1986.

Easen, P. *Making School Based INSET Work*, Open University Press, 1985.

Elliot, G. *Self-Evaluation and the Teacher*, Schools Council (mimeo), 1981.

Elliot-Kemp. *Staff Development in Schools. A Framework for Diagnosis for Identifying Teacher Development Needs*, Pavic Publications, 1981.

Gautry, T. *Lux Mini Laws: School board memories*, Link House, 1937.

Gough, R.G. 'Staff Development as part of the continuing Education of Teachers' in *British Journal of In-service Education and Training*, Volume 12, Number 1.

Grace, G. *Teachers, Ideology and Control: a study in urban education*, Routledge & Kegan Paul, 1978.

Grace, G. 'Judging Teachers: the social and political contexts of teacher evaluation' in *British Journal of Sociology of Education*, Volume 6, Number 1, 1985, pp.3–16.

Hancock, D. *Staff Appraisal in Schools and Colleges – A View from the DES*, Lecture to 'Education for Industrial Society', 25 February, 1985.

Hellawell, D. *Job Descriptions and Performance Appraisal*, Forthcoming article Education Dept., Birmingham Polytechnic Mimeo, 1986.

Inner London Education Authority. *Keeping the School under Review*, ILEA, 1977.

James, C. and Newman, J. 'Staff Appraisal: Current Practice in Schools' in *Contributions*, Number 8, Centre for the study of Comprehensive Schools, University of York, 1985.

Joseph, K. *Speech to the North of England Education Conference at Sheffield*, 6 January 1984.

Joseph, K. *Speech to the North of England Education Conference at Chester*, 4 January, 1985.

Killing, J.P.and Fry, N. 'Managing Change – pace, targets and tactics.' *Paper produced for IMEDE* (Institute pour L'Etudes des Methodes de Direction de L'Enterprise) Ouchy Lausanne, Switzerland, 1986.

Leigh, P.M. 'Ambiguous professionalism: a study of teachers' status perceptions' in *Education Review*, Number 31, 1976, pp.27–44.

McMahon, A., Bolam, R., Abbott, R. and Holly, P. *Guidelines for Review and Internal Development in Schools* (GRIDS), Longmans, 1984.

Miles, J. 'The Death's Head Trail to Teacher Appraisal' in *Education*, Volume 21, September, 1984, pp.235–6.

Montgomery, D. 'Teacher Appraisal. A Theory and Practice for Evaluation and Enhancement' in *Inspection and Advice*, Volume 21, Number 1, 1985, pp.16–19.

Montgomery, D. 'The nub is credibility' in *Education*, Volume 165, Number 12, 1985, p.259.

Moore, H. *Collected original resources in Education* (Core) Volume 10, Number 1, 1986, Carfax.

NAHT, *Staff Development: the appraisal aspect*, 1985.

Nias, J. 'Learning and Acting the Role: In-School support for Primary Teachers' in *Educational Review*, Volume 36, Number 1, 1984.

Nisbet, J. 'Appraisal for Improvement' in Dockrell et al., *Appraising Appraisal*, BERA, 1986.

Nottinghamshire LEA. *Teacher Professional Appraisal as Part of Development Programme*, Nottinghamshire County Council, 1985.

Nuttall, D. 'What can we learn from Research on Appraisals' in Dockrell et al., *Appraising Appraisal*, BERA, 1986.

NUT. *Teaching Quality*, 1984.

NUT. *Teacher appraisal and teacher quality*, 1985.

Oxfordshire County Council. *Starting Points* in *Self-Evaluation*, Oxfordshire Education Department, 1979.

Sharpe, R. and Green, A. *Education and Social Control: A study in Progressive Primary Education*, Routledge & Kegan Paul, 1975.

Shipton, D.G. *How are the Needs of Primary School Teachers to be Identified*: Unpublished Report of a Headteacher Fellowship, University of Warwick, Department of Education, 1987.

Sidwell, D.M. '*Staff Appraisal in Education: an analysis of practices and principles in UK, France, Federal Republic of Germany and USA*, unpublished MA Thesis, University of Warwick, 1987.

Slater, S.M. and Long, R.S. 'Whole School Evaluation: A Practical Guide for Senior Staff' in *Evaluation and Education*, Joint Issue 9/10 April, 1986, pp.37–67.

Solihull LEA. *Evaluating the Primary School*, Metropolitan Borough of Solihull, 1980.

Solihull LEA. *School Evaluation: A Guide for secondary schools* Metropolitan Borough of Solihull, 1986.

Stewart, V., and Stewart, A. *Practical Performance Appraisal*, Gower, 1977.

Suffolk LEA. *Those having Torches . . . Teacher Appraisal: A Study*, 1985.

Trethowan, D. ' . . . to appraise teachers, not to bury them' in *The Times Education Supplement*, 8 March, 1985, p.21.

Trethowan, D. *Appraisal and Target Setting: A Handbook for Teacher Development*, Harper & Row, 1987.

Turner, P. and Clift, P. *First Review and Register of School and College-Based Teacher Appraisal Schemes*, Open University School of Education, 1985.

University of Nottingham. *Managing Staff development in the Primary School: problems and strategies*, School of Education, Nottingham University, 1985.

Warwick, D. *Staff Appraisal*, Education for Industrial Society, 1983.

White, J. 'The end of the compulsory curriculum' in *The Curriculum* Institute of Education, 1982.

Wilcox, B. 'Context and Issues' in Dockrell et al., *Appraising Appraisal*, BERA, 1986.

Appendix 1

Extract from Evaluation Papers – Park Hall School

School Management and Review

Aims of Course

The Course will bring together the senior and middle management teams of the school. The Programme is designed to develop an understanding of the school as an integrated unit, within which management groups each carry out specific functions to aid the development of the school. During the Course we will explore the roles and responsibilites of senior and middle management and how these are interwoven in the running of the school. One of the major aims of the Course will be to develop an understanding of the approaches which can be used to review and evaluate the Department/Year in terms of successes and INSET needs. By the end of the Course we hope to have refined our school review process and developed a framework for action.

1. To develop an understanding of the school as an integrated unit, within which management groups each carry out specific functions to aid the development of the school.
2. To develop an understanding of the roles of the senior and middle management staff.
3. To develop an understanding of the approaches which can be used to review and evaluate the Department/Year in terms of successes and INSET needs.
4. To develop a co-operative framework for reviewing our performance and our in-service training needs.

Extract from Evaluation Papers – Abraham Moss High School

Management and Review

INSET Course – Group Targets

Group session 1 (Sat a.m.)

1. Elect a chairperson and secretary for the group.
2. Identify the major roles and tasks of a Head of Department.
3. Decide how a Head of Department can:
   (a) review their success in post;
   (b) determine the success of departmental staff;
   (c) establish the in-service training needs of individual staff and of the whole department.
4. What assistance can Senior Staff give in terms of departmental review and INSET?

Group session 2 (Sat p.m.)

1. Establish the major management roles of the Head of Year.
2. How can a Head of Year review his/her success in carrying out these roles?
3. How should the role of tutor be decided?
4. How can senior staff help in the process of review?

Group session 3 (Sun a.m.)

1. Complete unfinished tasks from Group Session 2.
2. Briefly, draw up a framework for reviewing the success and needs of department and year staff. Indicate how senior staff should be involved in this process.

Follow-up work

Identify what you feel are the INSET needs for:
(a) yourself;
(b) individuals in your department;
(c) the whole group (dept/team);
(d) whole school.

Appendix 2

Ways of Evaluating

We see at least three distinct ways of collecting information.

A. – Quantifiable Data

This type of data is the easiest to collect and is open to statistical analysis. Extreme care should be taken when using this type of data in isolation as other evidence should be gathered to enhance reliability. Quantifiable data is often open to hidden layers of error, e.g. we are all aware of the dangers of publicizing examination results without other information on the schools concerned – intake, resources, staffing, etc.

Examples of quantifiable data which may be useful

    (a)   pupil attendance which can be narrowed down into year groups or even tutor groups.
    (b)   staff attendance.
    (c)   external examination results.
    (d)   staffing – age structure, deployment on curriculum etc.
    (e)   capitation.
    (f)   punishments (pupil).
    (g)   pupil attainment.
    (h)   number of pupils receiving free meals/uniform grants etc.
    (i)   repairs to building.
    (j)   truancy.
          etc., etc.

Clearly there is a plethora of data which is available in school, either readily available or in need of collation. Additional information can often be gathered quickly by questionnaire. This type of data collection is often seen as non-threatening, especially if general information. However the more precise the data the more threatening it may become e.g. examination success in Mr X's class or attendance in Mr Y's, and staff absence are minefields.

B. – Self Evaluation Data

A large number of LEAs have issued checklists for teachers who wish to become involved in self evaluation. These checklists cover the classroom teacher, to the headteacher.

Clearly there are other methods of collecting data on one's own performance. These include: using a diary which provides a running, in-depth record of one's work, recording of lessons and then evaluating the result, the taking of notes during and after lesson, personal observation of specific parts of the lesson using a predetermined checklist/matrix. There are of course other methods which can be used by the teacher, however one must be clear about the questions one is asking, the data which will be collected and how it will be analysed and the effects on future action. The major criticism which can be levelled at self-evaluation data is its validity and reliability. The use of others in evaluation does enhance our chances of getting it right.

C. – Interpretive/Illuminative Evaluation Data

There are a number of approaches which fall into this area. We can group them into three categories:

1. The use of outsiders such as advisers, inspectors, H.E. staff, management personnel from industry, colleagues from other schools, etc. These outsiders need to be accepted and trusted by those being evaluated. Their roles and the areas in which they may act, must be clearly defined. Feedback from out-siders will need to be negotiated, perhaps modified before being accepted.

2. Group evaluation is often useful where team meetings are a regular feature of everyday life in the institution. By using these natural meetings we can harness a potentially strong evaluative function. It is in group meetings that plans for future action can be drawn up, tasks distributed and targets set. The extension of these meetings to include discussion and agreement of assessment/evaluative techniques for team tasks/targets is clearly necessary. Regular feedback sessions involving reports on progress, comments from the team, and the introduction of other data turns meetings into effective gatherings. Group evaluation may start with group or team targets to avoid threat and build trust and confidence before moving to individual target/tasks. The group meeting is also vital in

terms of clarifying roles and taken for granted assumptions about colleagues.

3. Evaluation by other colleagues in the institution. This can range from a geography teacher asking colleagues to observe his classroom practice to the head and deputy (curriculum) being asked to spend a week in the English department observing classroom practice, meeting and reviewing with the department the curriculum and resources. Where the decision is taken to use appraisal interviews as part of the process then a prerequisite must be classroom observation.

Extract from 'Whole School Evaluation and Staff Appraisal: A Practical Guide for Senior Staff' by S.M. Slater and R.S. Long, *Evaluation in Education*, 1984

Appendix 3

Staff Appraisal

Staff appraisal should be seen as an integral part of the overall programme of school evaluation. The process will be successful if a satisfactory climate has been developed in which there is mutual respect and trust between the reviewer and reviewee. The interview should be constructive, honest, supportive and not threatening to the individual. It should be considered supportive and challenging and be two-way, whatever the respective status of the parties involved. The appraiser will be under an obligation to provide professional development support to the appraisee whenever it is felt appropriate.

The general aim of staff appraisal is to improve quality within the education service. For individual teachers it should be to recognize, support and develop effective practices; to identify areas for development and to generate programmes for support and action.

Principles and practice of appraisal

If staff are to be encouraged or required to give of their best then opportunities must exist to provide discussion about their performance in relation to expectations. Staff must then receive feedback on both expectations and performance.

Teachers have the right to have access to whatever is written about them as part of the appraisal, and the right to respond or appeal. They have a right to expect a negotiated programme of professional development. Employers and those in authority also have a right to know what is going on in school/sections and a right to expect teachers to develop and expand their skills through professional development.

Who Appraises?

It is important to emphasize that there is more to appraisal than an appraiser going through a document with appraisee. Training for the appraiser is essential. Such training should come through a structured programme of professional development and be part of the staged programme mentioned earlier.

Who appraises whom will have been negotiated and decided within the school. There are a range of possibilities:

the headteacher being the sole appraiser;
the headteacher appraising senior staff and heads of section, followed by heads of section appraising their staff;
a school appraisal group, etc.

Schools will clearly decide what suits their own particular needs, however the principle should be that appraisal interviews are two way and developmental. All staff must be fully informed about the principles, practices and intentions of the programme.

Before the interview preparation

What is to be discussed at the interview may be decided in a variety of ways:

(a) an appraisal document containing a range of areas for discussion and used in all interviews;

(b) an appraisal document drawn up to relate to particular posts in the school;

(c) an appraisal schedule drawn up by the appraiser and appraisee prior to the interview and agreed by both;

(d) a 'pre meeting' to discuss the major areas to be tackled during the interview.

Prior to the appraisal interview time will need to be allowed for the gathering of information, and, as mentioned earlier, this should include classroom observation and observation of the teachers, in the context of their work. Part of this gathering of information will by necessity revolve around the teacher's job description/role responsibility. The appraisal process, including the stage of gathering information, should be positive and seek to identify the teacher's successes as well as identifying areas for improvement. The criteria for gathering information on which judgement may be made should be clear to all staff involved.

The interview

The climate must be such that a genuine exchange of opinions can take place. The interview must not be rushed and contingency plans should be made if there is insufficient time. The environment should be free from interruptions and allow for confidential discussions to take place. Attention should first be focused upon the review of past successes in the light of the information gathered and then on areas for improvement. Discussion should take place on the teacher's roles/responsibility and how this should be enhanced/supported in the future. The interview must give an opportunity for a two-way exchange of views and for an opportunity to discuss the appraiser's performance. During the interview both parties should agree on notes to be made, new targets to be set (which may be used as a focus for the next appraisal interview), and on future action in terms of areas such as INSET needs.

After the interview

A. There should be an opportunity to follow up the interview with any areas of concern which did not arise at the interview or where upon reflection new views are forthcoming.

B. The interview will need to be followed by action and the monitoring of this activity. The action will include monitoring progress towards new targets, or developing in-service training programmes. It is important that improvement is recognized and encouraged and this should be part of the school's evaluation process.

Appraisal interviews should be:

1. Part of the whole school evaluation programme.
2. Two-way and mutually advantageous.
3. Developmental.
4. Based on reliable information and criteria based observations.
5. Understood and supported by all those who are taking part.
5. Conducted within suitable surroundings.
7. Encouraging, supportive and challenging.
8. Periodic and always followed up.

Extract from 'School Evaluation – A Guide For Secondary Schools', unpublished draft document, Metropolitan Borough of Solihull.

Index

2 75561IT
17-10-88
Abp